THE LUTHERAN MANUAL

Junius Benjamin Remensnyder

www.JustandSinner.com

THE LUTHERAN MANUAL BY
JUNIUS BENJAMIN REMENSNYDER

Just & Sinner
1467 Walnut Ave.
Brighton, IA 52540

www.JustandSinner.com

ISBN 10: 0692202722
ISBN 13: 978-0692202722

TABLE OF CONTENTS

INTRODUCTION

Junius Benjamin Remensnyder (1841-1927) was a Lutheran pastor in Gettysburg, Pennsylvania, and served as the president of the General Synod of the Evangelical Lutheran Church from 1911 to 1913. Along with the present work, he authored *The Atonement in Modern Thought, The Post-Apostolic Age and Current Religious Problems, Heavenward: A Guide for Youth,* and *What the World Owes Luther.*

Remensnyder wrote *The Lutheran Manual* as an apologetic for Lutheranism within the diverse religious climate of nineteenth-century America. This work serves as a basic introduction and defense of Lutheran thought. He discusses such topics as the nature of worship, church polity, justification, piety, and the importance of Word and Sacrament. Remensnyder contends that the Lutheran church is both the most historic and the most Biblical of the Protestant churches. He cites several authors throughout the text from both Lutheran and non-Lutheran traditions in order to demonstrate the general Christian consensus on the benefits brought to the church through Luther's reformation.

To the modern reader this work will likely sound triumphalist. On every point throughout the work, Remensnyder contends for the superiority of the Lutheran church over all other branches of Christendom. It is apparent throughout the text that Remensnyder is not willing to admit the flaws one finds in Lutheran congregations, such as his contention that every single Lutheran pulpit contains explicit gospel preaching. This is not the case in the Lutheran church today, and neither was it in the late nineteenth century.

Despite his triumphalism, Remensnyder's work is an immensely helpful and instructive book on Lutheranism. He is very careful in his comparison of Lutheran beliefs and practices to those of Roman Catholicism and the prevailing Puritanical Protestantism of his day. For this reason Remensnyder's work is especially beneficial to those of the Reformed tradition, as well as to current Lutherans who are interested in learning what differentiates their church from others.

CHAPTER I.
THE NAME LUTHERAN.

AS the name Christian was first given the disciples of Christ in derision, so those who adhered to the pure gospel in the era of the Reformation were derisively styled "Lutherans." As Luther was the hero of the Reformation— the Providential agent of that blessed work— it was natural that those who clung to his doctrines should be associated with his name. Hence, as the Reformation spread throughout distant quarters of the world, wherever one would espouse the restored faith, the scornful remark would be made: "He is a Lutheran," and not only was it a mark of criticism, but also a badge of danger.

As the truth advanced however, and gained larger conquests, history repeated the lesson of old. For, just as had occurred with the term Christian, so it issued with Lutheran. That which had been applied as a label of ridicule, became a synonym of honor. Thus, while the Reformers used the official title: "The Evangelical (from *Evangelion*, the Greek word for gospel) Church," [1] in common parlance it was called "The Lutheran Church," and this popular title in practice has virtually supplanted the official one. This has been sometimes urged as objectionable. It is said by opponents that the Church of Christ should not be called after any human and imperfect person, no matter how illustrious. This would be true if it at all were meant to supplant the name Christian. But this it is not. It is first of all, as termed in the Scripture: "The Church of Christ;" "The Church of God;" or as called in the Apostles' and Nicene Creed: "The Holy

---

[1] Its usual title is 'Evangelical Lutheran Church;' 'Evangelical' being the name; 'Lutheran' the surname:" Schaff-Herzg Encyclopedia, Vol. II, p. 1370.

Catholic and Apostolic Church." In this primary and generic sense none other than a divine name dare be applied to it. But for practical uses, that the diverse phases of Christianity may be distinguished from one another, it becomes necessary to employ particular descriptive titles.

Such secondary titles, attached to the generic Christian name have accordingly become universal. Thus we speak of the Romanist, Episcopal, Presbyterian, Methodist, Congregationalism etc. churches, all of which secondary names are based upon merely human forms of government and administration. The name Lutheran is no more objectionable on the ground of finite limitations than any of these. But on the other hand, it has this incomparable advantage over all others, that it emphasizes and keeps in conspicuous view the pure evangelical doctrine which Luther confessed, and for fidelity to which he stood. This was illustrated in the noble response made by the Margrave of Brandenburg, who challenged for calling himself a Lutheran Christian, answered: "I was not baptized in the name of Luther: he is not my God and Savior; I do not rest my faith in him, and am not saved by him; and therefore, in this sense I am no Lutheran. But if I be asked, whether with my heart and lips, I profess the doctrines which God restored to light by the instrumentality of His blessed servant Luther, I neither hesitate, nor am ashamed to call myself a Lutheran. In this sense I am, and, as long as I live, will remain a Lutheran!'

Another benefit of using this name arises from Luther's unique and marvelous personality. "Luther," said the great Melanchthon, "is all in all, a miracle among men." Wrote Calvin: "Luther is the trumpet which has roused the world from its lethargy—it is not as much Luther who speaks as God whose lightnings burst from his lips." Says the great theologian, Dr. Dorner: "Luther was the first Christian of the modern world—one of those rare historical figures in which whole nations recognize their type." The eminent old Catholic, Dr. Dollinger, testifies: "It was Luther's over-powering greatness and wonderful many-sidedness that made him the man of his age and his people. His opponents were colorless and feeble by the side of his transporting eloquence. They stammered, he spoke." The secular historian, Froude, says of him:

"Luther's eyes were literally world-wide. Reading his Table-Talk, one ceases to wonder that this remarkable man changed the face of the world." The distinguished church historian, Dr. Schaff, writes of him: "No man—save the apostles—deserves so much to be held in grateful remembrance as Martin Luther, remarkable alike as a man, as a Christian, as a theologian, as a Bible translator, catechist and hymnist, as the bold champion of the freedom of conscience, and as the chief leader of the Reformation."[2] Wrote Carlyle: "I will call this Luther a true Great Man: Great, not as a hewn obelisk; but as an Alpine mountain. A right spiritual Hero and Prophet, for whom these centuries and many that are to come, will be thankful to Heaven."[3] The great critic Lessing uttered this high eulogy: "In such reverence do I hold Luther, that I rejoice in having been able to find some defects in him, for I have been, in fact, in imminent danger of making him an object of idolatrous veneration;" and even the Roman Catholic Count Stolberg feels compelled to bear this testimony to him: "Against Luther's person I would not cast a stone. In him, I honor, not alone one of the grandest spirits that have ever lived, but a great religiousness also, which never forsook him."

When Elijah was caught away in a chariot of fire to heaven, Elisha implored that a double portion of the mighty prophet's spirit might fall upon him, and so it is of incalculable benefit to the Church of Christ militant that the spirit of so unique a hero of the Lord as this should still inspire her columns. The faith, the reverence, the courage, and the keen spiritual vision of Luther, are what Christendom needs at all times, and what are specially required to meet the crises and perils of our day. And experience shows that the name Luther, attached to our Church, has kept his commanding figure at our head, and that its influence has been a constant and beneficial inspiration. Much of the unswerving loyalty of the Lutheran Church to the scriptures, and to the pure gospel of the

[2] Symposiac on Martin Luther, p. 21.

[3] Heroes and Hero Worship, p. 127.

Reformation, is owing to the manner in which the rare personality of Luther has perpetually been held up before her.

Whether then, we consider the name Lutheran, in its origin, or in the light of the history and achievements which three-and-a-half centuries have gathered about it, there is nothing in it to be defended, or apologized for, but it is a name to be proud of, and to inscribe boldly on our ecclesiastical banners. Other distinctive denominational names are empty and colorless by the side of it. No title is so fitted to awaken spiritual enthusiasm as that of the Evangelical Lutheran Church, and every worthy member of this great communion can say with a just pride: "I glory in the name Lutheran; so rich a heritage of spiritual blessing has this title bequeathed to our Church, that we cannot but believe that its selection was the handiwork of Providence."

CHAPTER II.
THE LUTHERAN AN HISTORICAL CHURCH.

THAT the purpose of God to bring salvation to the world might be carried out, He established the Church. Under the Old Testament dispensation this existed as the Jewish Church. At the coming of Christ it was transformed into the Christian Church. This Christian Church has undergone many changes, but never has it been destroyed. For about three centuries, during the era of the Roman persecutions, we speak of it as the Early or Primitive Church. Thence from the era of Constantine it gradually assumes the Mediaeval form, the Church of the Middle Ages. About the tenth century occurred the great schism between the Greek and Roman wings of the Church.

When the Roman Catholics contend that theirs alone is the one old historic Church, the answer is that the "Greek or Oriental Church is the oldest in Christendom, and for several centuries was the chief bearer of our religion. She still occupies the sacred territory of primitive Christianity, and claims most of the Apostolic Sees, as Jerusalem, Antioch, and the Churches founded by Paul and John."[4] She produced the first Christian literature and used the language spoken by Christ and His apostles. Did any branch of Christianity possess the exclusive claim to the descent from the original historic tree, it would then be the Greek rather than the Romish branch.

The great Reformation of the sixteenth century from which issued the Lutheran Church, did not originate any new thing. It was a Re-formation, not a creation. It only restored the old. It tore away the heap of Mediaeval rubbish of superstition and ceremonial under which the pure faith and simple ritual of the Church had been buried. It was by the study of the writings of the early Church fathers, as

---

[4] Dr. Seiss, in Ecclesia Lutherana, p. 34.

Augustine, etc., that Luther was largely led to break free from Romish error. And therefore his aim was to return to the purity of the Primitive and Apostolic Age. He simply built upon the old "foundation of the apostles and prophets, Jesus Christ Himself being the chief corner-stone." "That is exactly what we mean by the German Reformation, which was not a new development of Christianity, but simply the process of scraping off the barnacles that had been accumulating for fifteen hundred years, and more and more obstructing Christianity's progress through the midst of this storm-tossed world that it was set here to sail on."

Had Luther been a destructive radical, recklessly going on a career of innovation, he would not have been followed and supported by millions of the best and wisest of Christians. But he was a judicious conservative who revered the past. He knew that there had always been, and always would be, a true visible Church of Christ. Therefore he did not by any means break with the historical continuity of the Christian Church. When he renounced the Pope, this was not renouncing the true Church, but only declaring the more truly and loyally for it. So he and his followers never severed themselves from the ancient Christian tree, but the decayed and corrupt branches severed from them, and left them the representatives of pure historic Christianity. "Whilst Luther emended the gravest errors and vices of the Church of Rome, and restored the Church to a happier condition, he did not frame a new Church," says Budeus. "When the Lutherans renounced the Papacy and its abominations, they took with them the same Bible, the same Catholic Confessions, the same Holy Faith, and the same Apostolic Ministry and Sacraments, which distinguished the Church in the beginning, and hence the same historic Church-life, which took its rise in the incarnation of the Son of God, which trickled feebly through the rubbish and darkness of the middle ages, and which never was, or could be, entirely lost."

Had the Lutherans rejected anything simply because Rome held or used it—the position of some ultra-Protestants—they would thereby, to that extent have cut themselves off from the true visible Church. But whatever "of ancient Christianity, both in faith and usage, had come down through the middle ages, pure and incorrupt, they reverently and lovingly retained. And only that which was unscriptural and a perversion of the Gospel, did they reject. "The sacred treasure of true Catholicity, which the Church of early times had nurtured in the form of Greek-Roman culture, is taken over— freed from excrescences, and enriched by those acquisitions of the Middle Ages that had stood the proof. Its vocation was to set forth the happy mean."[5] This left the Lutheran not only a living branch, but the main trunk of the historical Christian Tree. It was not the Lutheran, but the Romish phase, which severed itself from pure primitive Christianity. If there was an apostasy, a falling away, from the Church of Christ in the Reformation, it was Rome, and not the Lutherans who were guilty of it.

And as, then, the Evangelical Lutheran Church is built upon the pure Word of God and Sacraments of the Lord Jesus Christ and His holy Apostles; and as her Ministry is descended in unbroken line from apostolic ordination; and as she retains the devout usages of the Church in her primitive purity; she is without doubt a true historical Christian Church. It is a fact capable of demonstration that no Church in Faith, Worship, and Order, is in such accord with the Church framed by Christ and the Apostles, as the Lutheran. With all charity and fraternal feeling toward Christians of other households we may yet truly say that to no other communion applies so fitly as to the Lutheran, the title: "The Holy Catholic and Apostolic Church."

In her we see in its most glorious and perfect form the visible kingdom of God—the gate to the holy Jerusalem and heavenly temple above. And he who adds himself to her membership may do so in the full confidence that in her is fulfilled this great investiture of the Lord Jesus Christ: "Upon this rock I will build My Church: and the gates of hell shall not prevail against it" (Matt, xvi: 18).

[5]Church History, Kurtz, Vol. Ill, p. 144.

CHAPTER III.
THE LUTHERAN CHURCH THE SOURCE OF THE OTHER PROTESTANT CHURCHES.

PROTESTANT and Lutheran were originally synonyms. It was the Lutherans alone who made the famous protest at Spire in 1529 from which they were called Protestants. And the indelible connection of this title Protestant with all the non-Romish Churches, serves to stamp them all as generically of Lutheran origin.

When Luther on the 31st of October, 1517, nailed his 95 theses to the doors of the Castle Church at Wittenberg, the act aroused the civilized world. Says a writer of that time: "The theses were transmitted to all parts of the earth as if the angels were their messengers." Luther's hammer awoke the slumbering nations. From his first stroke, the great Reformatory movement was begun, and Popes, Councils, and Princes, might as well have sought to turn the earth backward on its axis, as to attempt to retard its course. Everywhere Luther's books were in men's hands, and people were eagerly studying the new and yet old doctrines. In Switzerland, in France, and in England, these influences were most powerfully felt. The great Swiss Reformer, Zwingli, and the great French Reformer, Calvin, both thankfully acknowledged their indebtedness to Luther.

In England, especially, the movement made itself felt. "Luther's writings were eagerly read in England."[6] Indeed as early as 1521 official complaint was made to Cardinal Wolsey "that the University of Oxford is infected with the heresies of Luther, divers students having a great number of books of the said perverse doctrine." The same year Cardinal Wolsey issued a rescript

---

[6] Church History, Kurtz, Vol. II, p. 313.

condemning Luther's writings and ordering all copies to be delivered up within fifteen days. Notwithstanding these sharp measures, a noted writer of that time says: "Lutheranism increased daily in the University of Oxford." In 1526 appeared Tyndale's translation of the New Testament, evidently inspired by Luther's translation of 1522. An Episcopal writer admits of it that Tyndale "had Luther's translation before him and constantly consulted, and often adopted it." The same is true of the first authorized version of the whole English Bible by Coverdale in 1535. "The Origin of the English Bible is therefore," says Dr. Jacobs in his recent learned volume, "to be traced to German soil and Lutheran influences."[7]

Protestantism, however, as an organized ecclesiastical movement, dates its origin from the adoption of the Augsburg Confession, June 25th, 1530. From this time, it was no longer the individual work of Luther, but a purified phase of Christendom viz: the Lutheran Church. And this Augsburg Confession, which was wholly and distinctively Lutheran, laid the doctrinal foundation of all the other Protestant Churches. Says D Aubigne, the Reformed historian, of it: "The Augsburg Confession will ever remain one of the master-pieces of the human mind, enlightened by the spirit of God." [8] Writes the Presbyterian, Dr. Schaff: "The Augsburg Confession will ever be cherished as one of the noblest monuments of faith from the Pentecostal period of Protestantism.

Its influence extends far beyond the Lutheran Church. It struck the key note to the other evangelical confessions." And says Gieseler, the great Reformed Church historian: "If the question be, which among all Protestant Confessions, is best adapted for forming a union among Protestant Churches, we declare ourselves unreservedly for the Augsburg Confession." Dr. Krauth writes: "In it the very heart of the gospel beat again. To it, under God, more than to any other cause, the whole Protestant world owes civil and

---

[7] "The Lutheran Movement in England." Jacobs, p. 219.

[8] History of the Reformation, p. 497.

religious freedom." [9] And the scholarly Bishop Whittingham, of Maryland, speaking for the Protestant Episcopal Church, says: "The Augsburg Confession is the source of the Thirty-nine Articles of the Church of England and America— their prototype in form, their model in doctrine, and the very foundation of many of their expressions." [10] This is most natural, since the Thirty-nine Articles (Episcopal) were not adopted until the year 1563, when the Reformation had already been fought and won under the Augsburg Confession, which appeared thirty-three years, or a whole generation earlier. The Westminster Confession (Presbyterian) was not adopted until 1648, a full century later, and some of the confessions of the other leading Protestant Churches are quite modern. It was inevitable, therefore, that all these should have been substantially drawn from the Augsburg Confession, i.e. were Lutheran in their origin.

History, moreover, shows that the English Reformation was not only due directly to Luther and Lutheranism, but was on the very point of ecclesiastically joining the new movement. Soon after the adoption of the Augsburg Confession, viz. in 1535, an official English commission was sent to Wittenberg, where after lengthy conferences with Luther and Melanchthon, thirteen doctrinal articles were mutually adopted in which the King of England "agrees to promote the gospel of Christ and the pure doctrine of faith according to the mode in which it was confessed in the Diet of Augsburg." These negotiations after continuing for years, finally failed, and the Church of England was not amalgamated with the Lutheran Church. But not only did the essential identity of their confession remain, but their forms of worship were chiefly taken from Luther's service, and in America the Episcopal Church officially styles herself, Protestant, which as we have shown, historically signifies Lutheran.

[9] Conservative Reformation, p. 258.

[10] Lutheran Origin of the Thirty-nine Articles of the Anglican Church—Dr. J. G. Morris.

"Lutheranism was, in fact, the exact shade which colored the minds of Queen Elizabeth, and of the divines who held to her. Her altar was precisely the Lutheran altar: her opinions were represented in almost a continuous line by one divine after another down to our time."[11] The Lutheran belief of Elizabeth is shown by her noted words:

Christ was the Word that spake it,
He took the bread and brake it,
And what that Word did make it,
That I receive and take it.

In the face of these indubitable historical facts, how utterly groundless is the claim sometimes put forth that the Episcopal Church of England and America stands alone in this respect, that it is independent of the Lutheran Reformation, and has had a continuous existence from the apostolic time apart alike from the Romish Church, and from the great religious awakening of the sixteenth century! When Luther appeared, and the Lutheran Church arose, there was but one great ecclesiastical system dominating Christendom, and holding the civilized world in its grasp: the Roman Catholic Church. To Luther and the Lutheran Church, therefore, all the now existing non-Romish Churches owe their origin and their general character. And of all these Churches not one has been so directly dependent upon the Lutheran, and has so nearly reproduced it in doctrine and worship as the Episcopal.

The Lutheran Church then is without exception The Source of the other Reformed churches. To her belongs the proud title: "Mother of Protestantism." "The Reformation of the Sixteenth Century is the mother or grandmother of at least half a dozen families of evangelical denominations not counting the subdivisions."[12] And as daughters should venerate their mother, so

---

[11] Christian Institutions, Dean Stanley, p. 89.
[12] Schaff's Church History, Vol. VII, p. 9.

affectionately should the various Protestant churches regard and venerate her as "the rock whence they were hewn." "It is the truism of history that the Lutheran is the parent Evangelical Church. She is the mother of Protestantism. Historically all other Evangelical churches have sprung from her."[13]

---

[13] The Lutherans in America, Wolf, p. 505.

CHAPTER IV.
THE LUTHERAN CHURCH AND THE WORD OF GOD.

THE corner stone of the Lutheran Church is Holy Scripture. From the day that Luther found the Bible in the University at Erfurt, the Reformation was born. In that sacred volume lay the beginnings of the mighty movement that was about to recreate the world. It was by the study of the Word of God that Luther became enlightened as to the errors of Romanism, and it was with this sword of the spirit that he led forth the Church from her bondage, to the liberty and progress of the modern era. It was on the rock of the Holy Scriptures as over against the edicts of Popes and the decrees of Councils that Luther planted himself at Worms—that "scene" which Froude calls "the finest in modern history,"— when he uttered the memorable words: "Here I stand, I cannot do otherwise; God help me, Amen!"

Accordingly, Luther's first great work was to translate the Bible and place it, in the simplest language, in the hands of the people. Preaching, too, at once resumed the chief place from which it had been supplanted in the Mediaeval services. From Luther's own pulpit in Wittenberg and from Lutheran pulpits everywhere the Word of God resounded, as it did of old when Christ and His Apostles "came preaching the kingdom of God." And when the Augsburg confession was set forth as the chief symbol of the Lutheran faith, it was a mere republication of the teaching of Holy Scripture. Accordingly when the Roman Catholic Duke of Bavaria said to the theologian Eck: "Can you refute by sound reasons, this their confession?" "With the writings of the Apostles and Prophets—no," replied Eck; "but with those of the Fathers and Councils—yes." "I understand," replied the Duke, "the Lutherans according to you, are in the Scripture; and we are outside."

And this peculiarity still characterizes the Lutheran Church, not only as over against the Roman, but even measurably the Reformed Churches. The position of Lutheranism in respect to the Word of God is unique. In no Christian communion does it hold so unequivocally the place of absolute authority. Such was the reverence of Luther for the Bible that he does not scruple to say that we must look upon the Scripture as "if God Himself had spoken therein," and he calls the Holy Spirit "the most clear and simple writer there is in heaven and on earth."* And this same reverence has passed into the Church holding his name. For, while we gladly concede the * prominence which all Christian churches, Greek, Roman, and Reformed, give to the Scripture, yet the Bible does hold a special pre-eminence in the Lutheran Church, such as it has not elsewhere.

With it the Word of God is the chief Means of Grace. It is the source of the efficacy of the Sacraments. It is the seed of the spiritual life. It is the organ of our personal relation to Christ by which He lives in the believer. It is the instrument of sanctification, the formative power of growth in grace, "Sanctify them through thy truth, thy Word is truth" (Jn. xvi, 17). And it is the only infallible rule of faith and practice. The Word, therefore, in the Lutheran Church is the supreme and all sufficient spiritual agent. Nor is it held as necessary to its effect that it be attended with concomitant agencies and appliances of human wisdom and "human machinery." But rather do these supplant and enfeeble it, even as Oetinger complained that the followers of Zinzendorf placed more reliance upon the singing of his emotional hymns than they did upon the Word of God. For when simply and purely preached it exerts its utmost spiritual influence: "That your faith should not stand in the wisdom of men, but in the power of God" (1 Cor. ii, 5). It therefore is the staple of Lutheran preaching and the center of every Lutheran service.

No Church so closely molds its confessions, its theology, its liturgical services, its hymnology, its devotional literature, and its simple Christian life after the Scriptures, as does the Lutheran.

With her the Church stands by and depends upon the authority of Scripture, and not Scripture upon the authority of the Church. Emphatically among her ecclesiastical sisters may she wear the title: The Bible Church. Fitly thus does the historian Kurtz, term her: "The Church of the pure doctrine." And Dr. Schaff says of her: "The Lutheran Church meditated over the deepest mysteries of divine grace and brought to light many treasures of knowledge from the mines of revelation. She can point to an unbroken succession of learned divines who devoted their whole life to the investigation of saving truth."[14] The Lutheran Church accordingly has no sympathy with the low and loose views current in many Protestant quarters, respecting the sacred oracles. She does not consider the Bible as merely the imperfect record of a divine revelation, but she regards it as that revelation. She does not think that the Scriptures merely contain the Word of God, but that they are the Word of God. She does not view the Scriptures as a promiscuous intermixture of human error and divine wisdom, but as absolute and unmixed truth. To her the Bible is "The Word of God which lives and abides forever." (1 Pet. I, 23). For her the Bible is no book of man's origin, but in it she hears the voice of "God, Who at sundry times and in divers manners spoke in times past unto the fathers by the prophets" (Heb. i, 1). And therefore she does not receive the Bible with conditions and compromising qualifications, but she receives it as reverently as did St. Paul, to wit: "For I neither received it of man, neither was I taught it, but by the revelation of Jesus Christ" (Gal. i, 12).

The Lutheran Church does not then with one breath receive the Scriptures, while with the other she invalidates them by a low theory of inspiration, but to her they present "not the words which man's wisdom teaches, but Which the Holy Ghost teaches." (1 Cor. ii, 13). Therefore her position is that which Dorner quotes as that of Luther: "God in revelation is God in the Word. In the Word thou shouldst hear nothing else than thy God speaking to thee." Or as the great theologian, Gerhard, writes: "Although God did not directly write the Scriptures, yet it is God and indeed God alone, Who

---

[14] History of Protestant Theology, Vol. I, p. 107.

inspired the prophets and apostles, not only as they spoke, but also as they wrote; and He made use of their lips, their tongues, their hands, their pen."[15]

The Lutheran Church then regards the Scriptures as the revelation of God's Word and Will, and hence the one only infallible rule of faith and practice. By this standard, therefore, she frames her creed, molds her theology, and shapes her system of ethics. And with these high views of Scripture, she does not stumble at what that Word reveals. What God affirms she receives 'with implicit faith, believing that His power is equal to His word, and that what He says He can do. Hence she does not hesitate where the Scripture doctrine involves a mystery. But despite the arguments of the skeptical reason, and the sneers and taunts of infidels, "as a little child" she "receives with meekness the engrafted Word" (James i, 21).

As Luther, in the colossal bronze group at Worms, stands with the open Bible in his hand, and his face upturned to heaven— the noblest artistic impersonation of moral grandeur in the world— so does the Evangelical Lutheran Church stand upon the impregnable rock of Holy Scripture. And it is this Rock upon which, as a Lutheran Conference has recently declared in Berlin, "the wisdom of this world will be rent asunder."

[15] Schmid's Lutheran Theology, p. 69.

CHAPTER V.
JUSTIFICATION BY FAITH THE CENTRAL LUTHERAN DOCTRINE.

IF the Word of God, as the sole fountain of authority for the Christian conscience, as over against the authority of Popes and Councils, was the chief means of the Reformation, the doctrine of that Word most potent in the movement was Justification by Faith. This central truth of the New Testament, involving the very heart of Christ's Incarnation and redemptive work, had been lost sight of during the Middle Ages. Instead of teaching that the sinner was justified freely by faith in Christ's blood and righteousness, justification had been made dependent on human works and merits and narrowed to priestly intervention. Consequently a system of penances, indulgences, masses, repetitions, and monkish routine, had come in vogue, instead of simple spiritual piety. Not only did these heavily burden and oppress the conscience, but they placed a bar between the soul and its immediate living intercourse with the Savior. All Christendom was groaning under this intolerable perversion.

But when Luther had reopened the Bible, and studied it carefully for himself, he discovered this lost cardinal principle of Christianity. Especially one day, when on a pious pilgrimage to Rome, while, as a work of penance, climbing Pilate's staircase, the Pauline passage, "The just shall live by Faith," flashed upon his mind. Then it was, that he also saw the falsity and absurdity of this whole system of meritorious works. He realized that it was a total misconception of the gospel. That it was the servile routine of the slave and not the loving, joyous obedience of the Son. At this discovery a great burden rolled from Luther's soul. He saw that what all his monastic penances and self-mortifications failed to procure, was freely offered him through simple trust in the all atoning merits of the crucified Lamb of God. Then Luther for the first time experienced true and perfect spiritual peace. He had now, so to speak, found the key of the lost Paradise. And he now goes forth from his closet where God has made him a free man in Christ Jesus, to give this boon of spiritual freedom to the world.

Henceforth this becomes "the one central point in Luther's heart and life, in his theology and in the testimony of the Church called after him, namely, the clearness, firmness, and joyfulness, of that justifying faith which was, then, for the first time since the days of the apostles, restored in its fullness to the Christian Church." Wielding in his unique personality this vital Evangelical doctrine he broke the Papal bondage of a thousand years, reformed the corrupted Church of Christ, created a new historic epoch, opened the door of the modern era, and transformed the whole condition of man. That we are "justified by faith," that this faith introduces us into a personal union with Christ, and that this new spiritual life issues in good works—this pivotal gospel truth—is the explanation of all our unwonted modern progress. The superior enlightenment of Protestant over Romish nations, the greater spirituality and practical piety of Protestant peoples, and the unfettered advance of education, liberty, and the arts and sciences, since the reformation, are all owing to this vital evangelical principle.

And if this is the chief factor that differentiates Lutheranism from Romanism, it also to no small degree distinguishes the Lutheran from the Reformed Churches. For, while the Reformed Churches owe their origin to this same principle, and more or less hold and confess it, yet they by no means have the clear grasp of it had by the Lutheran Church. It does not with them hold the primary place that it does in Lutheranism, where it is, as Luther termed it, the *articulus stantis aut cadentis ecclesiae*, i. e. article of the standing or falling of the Christian Church. For example, in the Calvinistic system, while Justification by Faith has a place, it is yet made secondary to the absolute sovereignty and decree of God, which, without any sphere for man's voluntary action, is the sole cause of faith. "The Lutheran Church has always been a unit in the rejection of those gloomy errors which center in the theory of absolute election to faith. While she never swerved from the fundamental truth that salvation is by grace alone, she just as firmly maintained the other fundamental truth, that salvation is by faith alone, as the only means by which the soul can appropriate the merits of Christ."[16] "Anglicanism has sought to confine Christ's grace to narrow channels. Methodism often dims His crown by its conjunction of experiences and works with grace."* Lutheran theology on the other hand is Christo-centric. All revolves about Christ as the shining center. And as a matter of fact there is a wide spread degeneracy in much Protestant teaching in regard to this great central article of Justification by Faith. In how many pulpits is the death of Christ on the cross robbed of all its significance as a vicarious sacrifice, and reduced to a mere moral example. That He was the infinitely precious offering over against an infinite guilt of sin; that He by His suffering paid man's full penalty; and that we have remission of sins through His blood; is not only ignored but openly denied, and even represented as morally unjust and revolting. A far worse and more fatal error this than that Romish perversion against which Luther raised his protest!

And others, thoroughly evangelical in most respects, still misconceive and misjudge this great principle of Lutheranism. Thus, the late Canon Liddon speaks slightingly of "Luther's imputation doctrine," as one for which he had "no sympathy, as it often led to lax morality, etc.," and then adds condescendingly that "good Lutherans are always better than their theory."[17] Yet the Gospel does not fear that it will "lead to lax morality" when it makes salvation conditional on faith alone saying: "He that believes on the Son has everlasting life" (Jn. iii, 36). Nor was St. Paul fearful that this doctrine of Christ would lead to fruitlessness in good works, when he declared: "Therefore we conclude that a man is justified by faith without the deeds of the law" (Rom. iii, 28). This idea that the Lutheran doctrine fosters indifference to good works, whether urged by Romanists or Protestants, is an utter perversion both of Scriptural and Lutheran teaching. The Scripture teaches definitely and cumulatively that the ground of our justification is solely and absolutely the blood and righteousness of Christ, and that the

[16] Distinctive Doctrines and Usages of the Lutheran Church, p. 29

[17] Magazine of Christian Literature, March, 1890.

condition or means of our justification is faith which lays hold upon the great "propitiation for sinners." But this is not a mere intellectual assent, such as Canon Liddon speaks of, or Paul, when he says: "The devils believe and tremble." But it is a "Faith which works by love" (Gal. v, 6). A faith quickened by, aglow with, and fruitful unto love. And the outcome and test of this living faith are good works. The sinner forgiven much loves much. The greater the free love and pardon of Christ, the greater his impulse toward a life of grateful, good works. The new life born of faith is the Christ-life of love to God and the service of fellowmen. "By their fruits ye shall know them." And this vital Protestant principle has so illustrated its practical force in the moral regeneration of the world as to render quite superfluous any vindication of it.

Two fundamental departures from the evangelical tenet of justification are conspicuous in the Protestantism of today. One is that which disconnects Faith from its scriptural relation to the Church. For while Faith is the sole condition of salvation it is mediated through the Word and Sacraments. Saving faith is generated by the Holy Scriptures and nurtured by the Sacraments. That Faith is thus given through the Means of Grace, and not to be violently disjoined from God's historical instrumentality for salvation—the Church—is the true evangelical order.

The other current error is the position so frequently heralded from Protestant pulpits that doctrines, beliefs, and confessions have little or nothing to do with Christianity, that it matters not what a man believes, but only what he does. Life is made the all important thing, and Faith quite relegated to the background, as altogether indifferent. The Lutheran Christian sees here simply bald Judaism or Paganism. This is the inversion and invalidation of the Gospel teaching. "Believe in the Lord Jesus Christ and thou shalt be saved" (Acts xvi, 31) was the apostolic message. This preaching, which was "to the Greeks foolishness" and "to the Jews a stone of stumbling," carried with it "the power of God" and changed the face of the world. In the divine plan Faith precedes and orders Life. We are "justified by Faith," and the vital principle thus imparted, "works by Love" to the production of the new Christian life. Thus, what we believe we do, is the Christian answer to Jew, Pagan, and Infidel.

"The great thing in true Religion is the Faith—the Creed—the facts and doctrines on which the soul rests for peace and salvation. There can be no right Religion without a right Faith." [18] "Credo"—I believe—is the confession which lies at the very starting point of the Christian course.

The open and tacit assaults thus made upon this great material principle of the Reformation, show what vital departures are taking place from the Evangelical doctrines of Luther and the Reformers, and that the Lutheran must needs stand for the truth today as of old. As, then, the central doctrine of her theological system, the great distinctive article of her Church, and the root principle of all her works of practical piety, Lutheranism writes upon the banner which she holds up before a lost race this sentence— the very heart of the Gospel of Christ— "Justification By Faith."

---

[18] The Golden Altar, J. A. Seiss, D.D., LL.D., p. n.

CHAPTER VI.
THE SACRAMENTS IN THE LUTHERAN CHURCH.

SACRAMENT is the Latin form of the New Testament Greek word *"Mysterion"* whence comes our English word Mystery. The Sacraments thus denote the sacred mysteries of Christianity—the holiest ordinances of our religion. The two Sacraments—Baptism and the Lord's Supper—were instituted by our Lord Jesus Christ. The nature and intent of the Sacraments are thus defined in Lutheran theology: "They are holy rites, appointed by God, through which, by means of visible signs, grace is imparted to man."[19] That is, God has instituted the Holy Sacraments to convey renewing grace to the soul. In each Sacrament, therefore, there are two factors, the divine invisible gift, and the earthly visible sign. And the relation between the two is that the latter is the instrument, or means of the former. That is, the visible element is the vessel through which the invisible gift is conveyed and given, as it is written: "This treasure we have in earthen vessels" (2 Cor. iv, 7), Thus, in the Sacrament of Baptism the outward element is water, and the invisible grace offered or given through the water is spiritual washing or regeneration. So, in the Lord's Supper, the outward, or visible elements are Bread and Wine, and the invisible elements given through them are the Body and Blood of Christ.

These two elements are not to be confused or mixed together, neither are they to be separated one from the other. But they are to be connected by this sacramental union, viz. that one is the vessel, or means of the other. To get the invisible gift the outward element must be used. "What, therefore, God hath joined together,

---

[19] Doctrinal Theology of the Lutheran Church, Schmid p. 537.

let not man put asunder." The Sacraments thus are not mere figures or signs, but they are means of grace. What they signify they also convey. They are the earthly instruments of God's blessed spiritual gifts. And as they are the institutions of God, so man's faith or unbelief can neither make nor unmake them. It can but determine their effect. He who observes them with faith receives their grace to his unspeakable good, and he who observes them impenitently profanes their gift to his nameless hurt. "Religion [according to the Lutheran conception] is not the Puritan idea of God's Law, but the Gospel idea of God's Love. Yet God's love is not as loose as are the prevailing views of it. It has an appointed way of making men righteous. And this way is not a vague, individualistic influence of the Holy Spirit over men's impulses and emotions, but it is a way of definite and objective means of Grace through which alone the Holy Spirit ordinarily works. These means of Grace are His Word, which both regenerates and strengthens, and two Sacraments, one of which implants the new life, while the other feeds it. To Lutherans then, the Gospel of God's love, revealed in Christ and received through Christ's means of grace, is the sum and substance of all."[20]

Such is the Lutheran doctrine of the Holy Sacraments. It complies with the Scriptural teaching, which always unites divine grace with the outward sacramental elements. And it does no violence to our senses which show us that no change has taken place in the elements, which simply remain as before, viz. natural Water, Bread and Wine.

But this view of the Sacraments, as held by the Lutherans, we at once notice is clearly distinct from that held both by the Roman Catholics, and by the other Protestant Churches. The Roman Catholics mix the outward element and the invisible grace, saying that one is changed into the other. This view contradicts the evidence of the senses. And the other Protestant Churches violently disjoin and separate the invisible and the visible elements, for they deny that the latter are instruments of the former. They teach that the earthly elements are only figures or signs, and not means of grace, and thus

---

[20] The Lutheran Church, Rev. Theo C. Schmauk.

the participant receives no grace whatever through the sacramental elements. Whatever blessing he experiences at the time he receives through his mind or spirit, apart from the direct external use. This latter view contradicts the teaching of Scripture. It also deprives the Sacrament of all direct efficacy. And the question at once arises, if God did not mean them to be the instruments of any blessing, why did He institute them, and ordain their observance? But how much more natural it is to think that what divine wisdom and beneficence have set up with such solemn sanctions, are not empty signs, but richly filled vessels—are not utterly devoid of efficacy, but clothed with spiritual might and power. From this presentation, the incomparably purer, richer, and more Scriptural view of the Sacraments held by the Lutheran Church, than that held by either the Roman or Reformed Churches, will appear.

It is sometimes charged upon the Lutheran Church that she teaches Sacramentarianism, i.e. that the Sacraments will produce their effects without faith, or a worthy spiritual state, and that she exalts the Sacraments over the Word of God. Both these charges are fully refuted by our highest authorities. Article XIII of the Augsburg Confession teaches of the Use of Sacraments: "Therefore men must use Sacraments so as to join faith with them, which believes the promises that are offered and declared unto us by the Sacraments. Wherefore they condemn those who teach that the Sacraments do justify by the work done, and do not teach that faith is requisite 'in the use of Sacraments." The same views are constantly upheld by our representative theological writers. Thus, says that prince of Lutheran theologians, Chemnitz: "The efficacy of the Sacraments is not such as if through them God infused, and, as it were, impressed grace and salvation, even on unbelievers or believers."[21] So also, Hollazius: "The Sacraments confer no grace on adults, unless when offered, they receive it, by true faith, which existed in their hearts previously." All Lutherans urge the necessity of moral fitness for the Sacrament, and likewise attach all its efficacy to the Word of God. As Augustine

---

[21]Doctrinal Theology of the Lutheran Church, 550.

says the Sacrament is "the visible word," so our theologians teach that "strictly speaking there is but one means of salvation, which is distinguished as the audible and visible word."[22] It is as Luther says in the Catechism: "The eating and drinking, indeed, do not produce these great effects, but The Words which stand here."

The Lutheran Church, then, teaches so just and discriminating a significance of the Word and Sacraments that we may fitly apply to her the striking apothegm of Claus Harms, when in 1817 he raised the banner of evangelical Christianity against the devastating inundation of unbelief: "I. The Roman Catholic Church is a glorious Church; she holds and forms herself pre-eminently by the Sacrament. II. The Reformed Church is a glorious Church; she holds and forms herself pre-eminently by the Word of God. III. More glorious than either is the Evangelical Lutheran Church; she holds and forms herself pre-eminently by the Sacrament and the Word of God."[23]

This one point alone, the true scriptural teaching of the Lutheran Church respecting the Holy Sacraments, gives to her a pre-eminence in Christendom, clothes her with a lever of spiritual power, and makes her the custodian of an incomparable divine treasure, which, while it holds the promise of such great things for her future, should also stimulate inviolable devotion on the part of her members.

[22] Ibid—Quenstedt, p. 538.

[23] Kahilis' History of German Protestantism, p. 225.

CHAPTER VII.
THE LUTHERAN DOCTRINE OF BAPTISM.

LUTHERANS teach that Baptism, according to the Scriptures, is the initial Sacrament. It is the door of entrance into the visible kingdom of God. It is the seal of the new covenant of our Lord Jesus Christ. It is the gate of admission into the Holy Christian Church. It is the beginning of the Christian life. Accordingly it differs from the Lord's Supper in that it is administered but once, at the beginning of the spiritual life, whereas the Lord's Supper, as the sacrament of renewal, must be continually repeated.

Let us look at the Nature, Mode, and Subjects of Baptism, in the Lutheran Church:

I. Nature. Baptism as a Sacrament, illustrates the truths laid down in the last chapter. "By Baptism," says Article IX of the Augsburg Confession, "grace is offered." It is then no mere symbolic rite, but it is a means of grace, conveying to the subject the spiritual gift which it typifies. What is this Baptismal grace? The Scriptures answer: "Except a man be born of water and of the Spirit, he cannot enter into the kingdom of God" (Jn. Iii, 5). "Be baptized and wash away thy sins" (Acts xxii, 16). "According to His mercy He saved us, by the washing of regeneration and renewing of the Holy Ghost" (Titus iii, 5).

These and corresponding passages show that Baptism is the bodily application of water with faith, and that the divine grace therein offered is new spiritual birth, or regeneration, by the gift of the Holy Spirit. This is the Lutheran teaching, as Luther defines in the catechism: "When connected with the Word of God, it is a Baptism, i.e., a gracious water of life and a 'washing of regeneration' in the Holy Ghost." Baptism then is the sacramental rite instituted as the ordinary means of the beginning of the new spiritual life in the soul. Where there is a trinal application of water, with the words of

Institution, and a believing heart, there the Holy Ghost is outpoured to cleanse original and actual sin, and to recreate the personality in the divine image.

"Reason," indeed says Luther, "can never understand how Baptism is a laver of regeneration, but what God says is true whether my senses corroborate it or not. He is omnipotent and can fulfill His Word."[24] This Baptismal Grace is not conveyed magically, but only in accordance with the Scriptural conditions. It can, too, be lost, and assuredly will, unless "That good thing which was committed unto thee," thou "keep by the Holy Ghost which dwells in us" (2 Tim. i, 14). Very precious, rich, and comforting, thus is Baptism according to the Lutheran view, presenting a wide contrast to the superficial views too largely prevalent respecting this Holy Sacrament.

II. Subjects. Is this Sacrament to be administered alone to adults, or also to children? The Augsburg Confession gives this direct answer: "Children are to be baptized, who by Baptism, being offered to God, are received into divine favor." So also Luther writes: "We must declare it as a simple fact, that a child, which by nature is oppressed with sin and death, begins eternal life at the time of its Baptism."[25] That baptism of Children was the primary design and rule—adult baptism being the exception, in such cases where the Sacrament had been neglected— is shown by the general tenor and individual statements of Scripture, by the Apostolic Baptisms, and by the practice of the primitive Christian Church.

a. The analogy of Baptism to Circumcision in the Scriptures sustains the Lutheran view. Circumcision was the Old Testament rite of admission into God's covenant. Now, as it was administered to children at eight days old, the conclusion is irresistible that Baptism, ordained by Christ to take the place of circumcision, must also be designed for children. Where is the authority for supposing that little children who even "under the law," were admitted into the Jewish Church, should under the "new covenant" of "grace and truth," be excluded from the Christian Church? How directly contrary this

---

[24] House Postils, Vol. I, pp. 296 and 298.

[25] House Postils, Vol. II, p. 337.

would be to those tender words of Jesus: "Suffer the little children to come unto me, and forbid them not; for of such is the kingdom of God" (Mk. i, 14). And also to the declaration of St. Peter, on the Pentecostal day, when the Church was founded: "For the promise is unto you, and to your children" (Acts ii, 39).

b. The Household Baptisms of the apostles show the same. Thus, when Paul "baptized Lydia and her household" (Acts i, 15), and when the jailer was "baptized and all his" (Acts xvi, 33), or when Paul says: "I baptized the household of Stephanus" (1 Cor. i, 16), is it not manifest that the "household" and "all his," and like phrases, were specially meant to include the little ones of the domestic circle?

c. Primitive Church Practice. Origen, one of the most learned fathers of the early Christian Church, who was born in the year 185, when those would be living whose fathers could have witnessed the apostolic practice, writes: "The Church has received it from the apostles that infants are to be baptized." And what is altogether conclusive, is that in the year 252 an ecclesiastical council of sixty-six bishops convened at Carthage delivered the decision: "It is our unanimous opinion that baptism must be refused to no human being, so soon as he is born." Truly, therefore, does Dr. F. W. Conrad say: "The early Fathers of the Christian Church, including Irenaeus, Tertullian, Origen, Justin Martyr, and others, represent in their writings that Infant Baptism was a universal custom derived from the apostles, and the practice was continued in the entire Christian Church, with a few exceptions, for fifteen hundred years. Furthermore, inscriptions in the Catacombs of Rome, giving the ages of neophytes or baptized children, also demonstrate the fact that infant baptism was practiced after the death of the apostles, in the first centuries of the Church."[26] And the historian, Guericke, justly remarks: "Without some Apostolical tradition, it is wholly inconceivable how the claim of Baptism to an Apostolical origin could ever have gained such unhesitating assent, and been generally

---

[26] On the Lutheran Doctrine of Baptism, p. 133.

adopted even in the 2nd century."[27] The only objection urged against these cumulative testimonies is that a little child cannot have faith. But does not our Lord answer this, when He says: "One of these little ones which believe in Me" (Matt. xviii, 6). Luther interpreted this as an unconscious faith, discernible to God alone. Augustine argues that in the case of children: "The faith of the Church, represented by Christian parents or sponsors, takes the place of their own faith."[28] As, then, faith in the adult is necessary to salvation, but children can be saved without faith, so though faith in an adult be necessary to Baptism, yet children can be baptized, and receive baptismal grace, without conscious faith. And though Baptism is thus the ordinary means of the regeneration, of infants, yet those dying unbaptized are not lost. Lutheran theologians hold that not the want, but the contempt of the sacrament condemns. Our duty is bound by the sacrament, but God's grace is not thus bound. He can regenerate and save where and how He will. Infants dying unbaptized are saved. Those responsible for their baptism will be held answerable for the neglect.[29]

The New York Independent has lately shown, by carefully tabulated statistics of all religious denominations in the United States, that the proportion of Infant Baptisms in the Lutheran Church is more than twofold larger than that of any other Protestant Church. And the Watchman, a leading Baptist journal, remarks that this is owing to the Lutheran doctrine of Baptismal grace. Where there is no belief of direct spiritual efficacy in the sacrament of Baptism, it is quite natural that the rite should fall into neglect. This fact accounts for the alarming decadence of Infant Baptism among non-Lutheran Churches. The most powerful Presbyterian Church in New York City, and perhaps in the United States, with 2000 members, lately reported but 21 Infant Baptisms for the year. A very significant

---

[27] Christian Antiquities, p. 238.

[28] Neander's Church History, Vol. II, p. 670.

[29] See Luther's views on this interesting point fully cited by Krauth on Augsburg Confession, p. 63.

illustration this, that belief in a power of God in the Sacraments is necessary to maintain their observance.

III. Mode. The Lutheran Church practices Affusion, i.e., pouring or sprinkling. The mode of baptism is not positively indicated in Scripture. The Baptism of Christ in the Jordan seems to indicate pouring. And His baptism is so represented in the frescoes of the Catacombs, one of which is supposed to date from the second century. So also Peter's question: "Can any man forbid water, that these should not be baptized?" (Acts x, 47), certainly indicates the application of water to the subject, rather than the immersion of the subject in the water. A very important testimony as to the practice of the primitive Church is that given in the recently discovered "Teaching of the Apostles," a book dating from a time quite as old as the formation of our New Testament canon. It says: "If thou have not living water, baptize into other water; and if thou canst not in cold, in warm. But if thou have not either, pour out water thrice upon the head into the name of Father, and Son, and Holy Spirit."[30] This proves beyond a doubt that either immersion or aspersion was considered a legitimate mode. That is, the amount of water was not deemed an essential factor of Baptism. Only those features of the Sacrament which were capable of universal use were made absolute. But the mode, depending upon conditions of climate and of the subject, as for example, whether sick or well, was left open for adaptation. Thus immersion, which could be safely used in a mild country like Palestine, but would be impracticable in a rigorous one like Russia, was not designed to be an essential feature of the rite. But, as pouring or sprinkling can be used in all countries and under all conditions, it has, with legitimate authority and judicious propriety, come into well-nigh universal use. And this is the mode practiced in the Lutheran Church.

[30] Ante-Nicene Fathers, Vol. VII, p. 879.

CHAPTER VIII.
THE LUTHERAN DOCTRINE OF THE LORD'S SUPPER.

THE most solemn institution founded by Jesus Christ, the most important public ordinance of the Christian Church, and that doctrine which has excited deeper interest and graver discussion than any other in theology, is the Lord's Supper. And it is just this holy and weighty doctrine which has become more distinctive of Lutheranism than any other. In fact, as over against the other Protestant denominations, it may be called the corner-stone of the Lutheran Church. For the view of the Lord's Supper which she holds and confesses, in harmony with the saints of old, has been either lost sight of, or definitely repudiated by the great majority of other Protestants. This view has been fitly termed The Real Presence. It is thus defined in Article X of the Augsburg Confession: "In the Lord's Supper the Body and Blood of Christ are truly present under the form of bread and wine, and are there communicated and received." It will be seen that two objects are here spoken of as being present in the Lord's Supper. One is the Body and Blood of Christ, the other is the Bread and Wine. The Body and Blood are the invisible divine element, the Bread and Wine are the visible earthly element. And the relation of the two elements is that the earthly is the means of the heavenly. That is, by using or appropriating the Bread and Wine the Body and Blood of Christ are received and appropriated by the communicant. The one is not changed into the other, so that the divine and earthly elements are confused—which is the Roman Catholic error of Transubstantiation. Nor are the divine and earthly separated, so that the Body and Blood are not received where the Bread and Wine are taken—which is the error of the other Protestant Churches—but the two are combined in an inseparable and yet unmixed union. This is called the sacramental union. And it is precisely in harmony with what we have shown to be the meaning of a Sacrament, viz. an invisible grace conveyed through a visible, earthly vessel. Now let us look at the reasons which prove this Lutheran doctrine of the Real Presence to be the only true one. Matthew, Mark, and Luke, all relate that on the evening of our Lord's betrayal He took bread and wine and declared of them these words: "Take eat: This is my Body," — "Drink: For this is my Blood." To St. Paul, also, the Lord after His ascension appeared and uttered the identical words of this sacramental formula. As Dean Stanley therefore says of this fourfold iteration: "These famous words form the most incontestable and authentic speech of the founder of our religion."[31] Now, the plain, natural meaning of these words is that Christ in the Holy Supper gives us His Body and Blood to eat and to drink. And the only question between Lutheran Christians and others is whether He meant what He said, or whether He did not mean what He said. and every error, which in any way mixes and confuses the divine grace with the earthly means, or which makes Christ's corporeal presence a carnal or physical one, she holds, that after a heavenly and incomprehensible manner, her Lord makes true His word, and gives to His believing disciples in the Holy Supper, His Body as the Bread of their spiritual life, and His Blood for the remission of sins.

The chief argument advanced to maintain the opposite view is that our Lord's words were figurative. But it is a rule of Scripture interpretation that no revealed word must ever be interpreted figuratively, where the direct natural meaning is admissible. On any other principle all the truths and doctrines of Scripture could be frittered away into tropes and figures, and no positive revelation would be left. And it seems quite inconceivable that in this most solemn scene, and with these words so precise and definite, and given us in fourfold repetition our Lord could have been disguising His meaning in symbolic language. "To suppose that at such a holy time

---

[31] Christian Institutions, p. 95.

as this He spoke in metaphor, is contrary to the solemnity of the occasion, the meaning of the institution, and the short, precise phrases employed." [32] St. Paul had no conception of a merely figurative significance, when he challenged unbelief on this very point thus: "The cup of blessing which we bless is it not the communion [participation in,' as the Revised Version margin literally renders it] of the Blood of Christ? The Bread which we break, is it not the communion of the Body of Christ?"[33]

For a Lutheran, the incontestable word of Scripture is sufficient. Yet to make the certainty more indubitable, we have the unbroken witness of the Church down through all the ages. Thus Irenaeus (130 A.D.-202), writes: "When the mingled cup and the broken bread receive the words of God, it becomes the Eucharist of the Body and Blood of Christ." Ambrose: (340-398) "We, receiving of one bread and of one cup, are receivers of the Body of the Lord." Chrysostom: (344-407) "The Bread which we break, is it not the communion of the Body of Christ?" So unanimous is this concurrence that the Church historian, Ruckert, says: "That the Body and Blood of Christ were given and received in the Lord's Supper, was, from the beginning, the general faith. No one opposed this in the ancient Church, not even the Arch-Heretics."[34] And Luther gives this powerful sentence in regard to it: "This article [the Real Presence] has been unanimously held from the beginning of the Christian Church up to this year 1500, as may be shown from the writings of the fathers, both in the Greek and Latin languages—

---

[32] Schaff-Herzog Encyclopedia—Lord's Supper, Vol. II, p. 1345.

[33] The Greek critical scholar, Alford, thus comments on this passage: "Κοινωνία, the participation of the Body and Blood of Christ. The strong literal sense must here be held fast as constituting the very kernel of the Apostle's argument. If we are to translate this as represents, or symbolizes, the argument is made void."

[34] Lord's Supper, p. 297.

which testimony of the entire, holy Christian Church ought to be sufficient for us, even if we had nothing more."[35]

With Lutherans philosophical objections to this doctrine are destitute of weight. We believe that God's power is equal to His Word, and that what He says, He can also do. We are only asked to believe the fact, the manner is and remains incomprehensible. We have but to do with the What? We must leave to God the How? The sacramental union of the divine and earthly elements is indeed a holy mystery, but no deeper or more impenetrable than the Incarnation, or the Resurrection, or the Trinal Unity. We have but to do as Thomas á Kempis so fitly counsels: "Human reason is feeble and may be deceived; but true faith cannot be deceived. Thou oughtest, therefore, to beware of curious and unprofitable searching into this most profound sacrament, if thou wilt not be plunged into the depths of doubt. But go forward with simple and unquestioning faith, and with reverence approach this holy sacrament, and whatsoever thou art not able to understand, commit without care to Almighty God."[36] Where there is this childlike Christian temper, there will be no difficulty in receiving the Scriptural and Lutheran view of the Lord's Supper.

The difference in the reverence for the Sacrament, and in its practical spiritual efficacy to the communicant, where the altar is approached with these strong, rich views, or where it is considered a mere sign and empty ceremony, is incalculable. To the latter it is but the memorial and shadow of a dead Christ, to the former it is a blessed communion with the living and glorified Christ. To the former it is like the mirage of the desert which invites and then disappoints the thirsty traveler; to the latter—partaking with a believing heart—it is a veritable fountain, whence the Real Presence flows out transmuting all the landscape into living green, filling the air with the carols of hope and the fragrance of joy, the soul irradiated and entranced by "finding Him whom it liveth."

[35] Letter to Albert of Prussia.

[36] Book IV ; Chap. XVIII.

The Real Presence is the peerless jewel of the Evangelical Lutheran Church. No other Protestant confession now professes to teach it. Of the thirty-nine Articles of the Church of England, for which the claim is sometimes made, Dean Stanley truly says that in them "the lion of Lutheranism and the lamb of Zwinglianism lie side by side, and it is well that they thus consist, or they could not mutually subsist."[37] Rejecting Transubstantiation, Consubstantiation, Impanation, and every error, which in any way mixes and confuses the divine grace with the earthly means, or which makes Christ's corporeal presence a carnal or physical one, she holds, that after a heavenly and incomprehensible manner, her Lord makes true His word, and gives to His believing disciples in the Holy Supper, His Body as the Bread of their spiritual life, and His Blood for the remission of sins.

To bear witness, in the very heart of Protestantism, to this central truth, she has never wavered during three and a half centuries, and never will, by God's help, to the end of time. And the significance of this stand of the mother, and greatest Church of Protestantism, cannot be over-estimated, in its bearing on the Christian world. It deprives Romanism of its most powerful shibboleth against Protestantism, viz. that it has emptied the blessed Sacrament of its spiritual efficacy. It anchors Lutheranism -safely in the conservative faith of the whole Christian Church as over against the deadly inroads of modern Rationalism.

And it augurs more than anyone can forecast for the future. Negations are barren, positive beliefs grow. After all—amid the mutable fashions and vagaries of transient times—truth abides regnant, the one ever advancing and dominant force on earth. And most of all does this hold in things spiritual. With, then, this far reaching truth of the Real Presence, lost from the coronet of her Protestant sisters, but glittering a peerless jewel on her brow, the Lutheran Church will go forward with an incalculable vantage. More and more will theologians be won to her doctrine, and devout

---

[37] Christian Institutions, p. 92.

Christians rally to her side, and more and more thereby will she become the recognized leader in God's witness-bearing Church to mankind.

CHAPTER IX.
LUTHERAN CHURCH POLITY, OR GOVERNMENT.

SINCE the Scriptures prescribe no definite form of Church organization, the Lutheran, being pre-eminently a Scriptural Church, does the same. Ecclesiastical order she holds to be a matter of freedom, to be determined by the varying exigencies of the occasion. While doctrine pertains to the conscience, order pertains to expediency. Accordingly, Lutheran Church Polity, or Government, is different in different countries. In Denmark, Sweden, Norway, Finland, Iceland, and Transylvania, it is Episcopal, the Church being under the government of Bishops and Arch-Bishops. And that the Lutherans in Sweden have what is called the "historic episcopate" is admitted by Episcopalians, as the Bishop of Connecticut writes of "Swedish Orders": "If anything outside the domain of pure mathematics may be said to be capable of demonstration, the reality of the Swedish succession is demonstrated."[38] In Germany, again, the Lutheran Church is under the administration of Superintendents, Consistories, etc. In America, the form of Church Constitution is Synodical, and many congregations are entirely independent.

The idea of the universal priesthood of all believers has overthrown in the Lutheran Church the doctrine of a distinction of essence between clergy and laity. The ministry is not an order, but it is a divinely appointed office, to which men must be rightly called. No imparity exists by divine right; an hierarchical organization is unchristian, but a gradation may be observed, (bishops,

---

[38] The Historic Episcopate in the Lutheran Church, Lutheran Quarterly.— Manhart.

superintendents, etc.) as a thing of human right only. In Sweden the bishops embraced the Reformation, and thus secured in that country an "apostolic succession" in the high-church sense; though, on the principles of the Lutheran Church, alike where she has as where she has not such a succession, it is not regarded as essential. The ultimate source of power is in the congregations, that is, in the pastor and other officers, and the people of the single communions."[39] Similarly writes Kurtz of the Constitution of the Lutheran Church: "The biblical idea of a universal priesthood of all believers would not tolerate the retaining of an essential distinction between the clergy and the laity. The clergy were properly designated the servants, ministry, of the Church, of the Word, of the Altar. Hierarchial distinctions among the clergy were renounced, as opposed to the spirit of Christianity. But the advantages of a super-ordination and subordination in respect of merely human rights, in the institution of such offices as those of superintendents, provosts, etc., were recognized."[40]

In this view of Church Polity, and ecclesiastical orders, the Lutheran Church has the support not only of Scripture, but of the Ancient Church. Thus, says the great father Augustine [354-430 A.D.]: "The office of bishop is above the office of priests, not by authority of the Scriptures, but after the custom of the Church."[41] And the foremost scholars of the Church of England have frankly admitted the same. Thus, writes the learned Bishop Hooker: "It is rather the force of custom, whereby the Church doth still uphold, maintain and honor the bishops, than that any such law can be shown that the Lord himself hath appointed presbyters to be under the regiment of bishops." [42] Church Government, then, in the

---

[39] Conservative Reformation—Krauth, p. 153.

[40] Church History, Vol. II, p. 363.

[41] Ecclesia Lutherana, p. 108.

[42] Ecclesiastical Polity, Book, VII, Chap. V.

Lutheran system being free, it is only a matter of human judgment and wise discretion what form it is best to adopt. Some form, however, there must be. For history shows that the progress, prosperity, unity, and efficiency of the Church, are quite as much affected by wise or foolish, orderly or anarchical, loose or efficient government, as civil states and societies are. In the United States quite too little attention, hitherto, has been given this important matter, so that the administration of the Lutheran Church is here perhaps the least orderly in the world. In fact, our point of weakness here lies in the sphere of organization. And from no other single cause, has our efficiency been so much crippled, and our progress been so greatly impeded. "We need order," the distressed cry of the patriarch Muhlenberg as he saw the distracted state of the American Lutheran congregations, is still reechoed on every hand. Order, oversight, judicious administration, a general superintendence of pastors and congregations, is one of the most intensely practical questions of the times. Our mighty Lutheran hosts are too much like a great, undisciplined, disorganized army, so that their overwhelming force cannot be utilized as it should be, cannot be moved by a common impulse, or brought to bear to a common end and purpose. In a recent paper on this point, a theological professor of large experience makes these judicious remarks: "Our convictions on this subject have been deepened more from the practical, than from the theoretical side. Life in the seminary makes many revelations concerning the needs of our congregations and the modes of supplying them, that are most surprising. We have most excellent material that admits of a high development, if we only treat it properly. But we are constantly losing some of the very best of it, because of our neglect to avail ourselves of the most simple and reasonable business-like methods with respect to its external administration. The question of greatest importance in our Church in this country at present, is that of its thorough organization upon the foundations laid for it by Muhlenberg. The indifference to more thorough organization for the efficient administration of the means of grace, is only a symptom of general religious indifference. If the Lord has actually given us a work to do, He means that we should do it with the most thorough adjustment of all our resources for its execution."

What the form of government of the American Lutheran Church shall be, is yet in the crucible of discussion and experiment. The growing tendency would appear to be toward a superintendency similar to that in Germany. Others think that a government by bishops, after the order of the one in Scandinavia, which has so efficiently preserved the unity and greatness of our Church there, would be the best.[43] A recent able editorial in the Lutheran Observer, while guarding carefully against any such Episcopate as would compromise the Lutheran doctrine of the universal priesthood and justification by faith alone, remarks: "That some kind of an 'episcopate,' or its equivalent in some form of adequate supervision, would be an advantage to the Lutheran Church of this country, is believed by many who think that the general work of the Church could be carried on more systematically and efficiently under such a form of administration, than under the present methods.

We think if the President of every Lutheran Synod could devote his entire time and labor to a general supervision of the Churches within its bounds, it would be a kind of an "episcopate"

---

[43] It is certainly a noteworthy fact, deserving the thoughtful reflection of every lover of his Church, that alone in Scandinavia of all Christian countries do we find the blessed phenomenon of practically but one Church—the Evangelical Lutheran. Thus in Sweden there are but 600 Roman Catholics, 30,000 Baptists and Methodists, and nearly 5,000,000 Lutherans! What might possibly have not a similar government done to prevent the distractions and divisions of Germany?

that would suit the situation and promote the progress and welfare of the Church." Had it not been, indeed, for the exigencies of the Reformation, Luther would doubtless have preserved ecclesiastical administration by bishops. He wrote: "The Church can never be better governed, and preserved, than with an Episcopal government, after the pattern of the Apostolic and Primitive Church."[44] But as Luther found that the Bishops personally were opposed to the Reformation, and that their power was, the bulwark of the Papacy, therefore, as the truth is greater than order, he wisely sacrificed the latter to preserve the former. The great historian, Neander, writes of the early Church that when the "contentions of parties" were proving "injurious to discipline and good order in the Churches, the triumph of the Episcopal system undoubtedly promoted their unity, order, and tranquility."[45]

All this shows the vital importance of some judicious, adequate form of Church government. To this end, it seems necessary to have some official Head or Executive, charged with the oversight of synodical congregations. And it would seem necessary that this person should be detached from individual congregational care, or at least have an assistant. He should be free to inspect and overlook the whole field, so that where counsel is needed, counsel can be had; that when difficulties arise someone may have time and ability to adjust them; that inexperienced young pastors may be admonished and guided; and so that instead of helmless drifting and confusion, there may be prudent, wise, and orderly administration.

While in theory, then, and in practice, the Lutheran Church must maintain pure doctrine as the essential characteristic of the Church, it is also a matter of the gravest practical moment, that there be an efficient Church Polity. That Polity is to be as variable as are the exigencies of the case. And that one—whether by a system of Synodical Superintendents or of Bishops—should be chosen, which

[44] The Episcopate for the Lutheran Church in America—Kohler, p. 15.

[45] Church History, Vol. I, p. 193.

is best adapted to the particular situation. It is admitted on all sides, that as our Church in America is growing so large and embracing such vast interests, the question of a government which will contribute to its wiser administration, order, unity, and efficiency, becomes every day the more pressing a problem of the hour. And this question should be met intelligently, patiently, and unselfishly, that under the guidance of Providence, our Church in this land may be so organized and ordered, as the most fully to develop its spiritual agency, as an efficient part of the universal Christian Church.

But in its discussion every true Lutheran will bear in mind the noble words of Bishop Von Scheele of the Swedish Lutheran Church, which sound the key-note to the Scriptural and Lutheran theory of Church government viz.: "It does not matter so much whether we have Bishops or not, but that we have Christ with us and confess Him, as the great Head and Bishop of the Church."

CHAPTER X.
LUTHERAN WORSHIP.

THE foundation of the ritual of the Lutheran Church was laid in Luther's work: "The Order of Service in the Church" (1523). It was his intention to retain all that was good in the service of the Catholic Church, while discarding all unevangelical doctrines and practices. The various states of Germany have their own Church orders, which differ, however, only in minor particulars. Luther introduced the use of the vernacular tongue into the public services, restored preaching to its proper place, and insisted upon the participation of the congregation in the services, declaring "common prayer exceedingly useful and helpful." The popular use of hymns was introduced by Luther, who was himself an enthusiastic singer, and by his own hymns became the father of German Church hymnology, which is richer than any other. Congregational singing continues to form one of the principle features in the public services."[46]

The foregoing is a very fair summary by an impartial witness, the Presbyterian Dr. Schaff, of the chief outlines of Lutheran Worship. It specifies these cardinal features:

1. That Preaching forms the central element of the service.
2. That "Common Prayer [Luther's own words] as exceedingly useful and helpful," is to have a leading place. That is, the minister is not to have the whole service to himself, but the people are to have their share in the worship.
3. That congregational singing is to be a "principal feature."

---

[46] Schaff-Herzog Encyclopedia, Vol. II, p. 1372.

4. That the services of the Ancient Church— the usages of Christians of all lands and times— were to be "retained," only "excepting unevangelical" features.

5. That there is a definite historical Lutheran service, which, while uniform in any particular country, "differs" in various states, "however only in minor particulars."

The remark often made that Lutherans in Europe have numerous varying orders of service is here seen to be essentially misleading. For, not only are these orders all framed after the same generic pattern, but only one uniform service is used in each different country or territory. Hence, Dr. Schaff's statement, as an unbiased judge, is quite correct.

As Luther reformed but did not destroy the old faith, so, also, he reformed and cast anew, but did not destroy the old service. Upon this venerable edifice of Christian worship, as the outgrowth, under the Holy Spirit, of Christian experience, and as the visible expression of the communion of saints, Luther would have been the last to lay irreverent or destructive hands. Of its origin and antiquity, Dr. Wenner well and beautifully says: "It is fair to assume that during the first century the principal outlines of the Christian Service were established and generally observed," indicating "an original impress of Apostolical usage and authority. Its foundations were laid in the far off past. Its object is the glory of God and the salvation of men. Its walls have breasted the storms and tumults of passing ages. Its architectural lines have continually pointed upward to the unseen world. The history of Christian Worship leads us on hallowed paths; to understand and behold its secrets we need anointed eyes. Many questions that agitate the Church at this time are of passing and relative importance. This affects its very life. It springs from the very heart of Christianity, and is intimately connected with the life of every believer."[47] As thus the Primitive and Mediaeval Church had been liturgical, and as Public and Common Worship, are impossible

---

[47] Christian Worship.—Lutheran Quarterly, October, 1892, pp. 452, 455

without common forms for the congregation, so also is the Lutheran Church liturgical. And that the Lutheran liturgy which Luther molded retained the leading characteristics of the worship of all the saints back to Apostolic times, is no reproach to it, but one of its chief glories. Who does not feel his faith strengthened and his religious devotion stirred by the consciousness that the prayer or song he is uplifting has voiced the devotions of the saints up to the throne for a thousand years! What a sublime illustration is this of Christian Unity! What a sweet and comforting realization of the communion of the saints! What a foretaste in the worship of the earthly temple of that in the heavenly temple, when in answer to a voice that came out of the throne there was returned the common response, "as it were the voice of a great multitude, and as the voice of many waters, and as the voice of mighty thunderings, saying, Alleluia; for the Lord God omnipotent reigns" (Rev. 19:6). There is no worship in the world to-day at once so ancient and so modern, so liturgical and yet so spontaneous, so reverent, and yet so stirring the deepest springs of living enthusiasm, as that of the Lutheran Church. Writes President White of Cornell University of Lutheran Worship in Germany: "These hymns laden with the highest hopes and inspirations of past centuries, take hold upon the German heart to-day. In the Churches the service of praise comes from the hearts and voices of the whole congregation." [48] And writes another non-Lutheran of Lutheran Worship in Berlin: "What pure, single worship is here! With all the liturgy and ceremony there is still a wonderful simplicity. There is a solemnity and beauty in its worship, an earnestness and reverence within its sacred temples, a richness, depth, satisfaction in its services—a reverence, in all, that fills the soul with a completeness of devotion. How one grows to love the Protestant Church of Germany."

The liturgical service of the Lutheran Church is eminently Scriptural, largely using the identical Scripture words; it places the preaching of the Word in the center about which all revolves; it is so

[48] Hand Book of Lutheranism, p. 15.

simple that a child or stranger can easily use it; and it is very brief, requiring only about one-fourth the time to the sermon occupied by the service of the Episcopal Church. Yet it is liturgically symmetrical and full. As a service for devotion, it is ordered in perfect adaptation to the nature of Christian Worship. It prepares the worshipper for the divine audience by the Confession; it begins the service proper in the Introit; it mounts to rapture at the beatific vision in the Gloria in Excelsis; it bows in prayer in the Collect; it hears the voice of God in the Epistle and Gospel; it returns the answer of the congregation in the Creed; it gives wing to Christian Song in the Hymns; it renders the sacrifice of praise in the General Prayer, and of gifts in the Offertory; and then it departs with the trinal Benediction. The service is responsive; is framed about the Christian year; is constantly varied, the Introits and Collects changing for every Sunday; gives preaching the central place; allows room for the exercise of liberty, as in the use or disuse of parts and in the choice of written or extemporaneous prayer; and is so simple and direct that any stranger can at once use it. "All its various parts center around Christ, presenting Him in all His offices, in both His states, in the fullness of His work, and in all His relations to the sinful and sorrowing, the penitent and believing, the afflicted and tempted, the dying and the glorified. Its lessons, and responses, and collects, and chants are intended simply to carry the devotions of the worshippers to the Throne of Grace, as far as possible, in the very words of Holy Scripture.[49] Wherever introduced

[49] That able and moderate journal, the New York Observer (Presbyterian), thus speaks of this feature: "To many devout persons this Lutheran Service-Book will be chiefly interesting and acceptable because of its Scriptural character, a large part of its phraseology being in the language of sacred writ, the Psalms and Lessons being given in the incomparable English of the Version which has been more widely read than any other words that ever were written. * * * Perhaps the most remarkable thing about this service is that it is not commanded, but commended to the use of the Churches for which it was provided. So careful are the Lutherans of the liberty of the people in matters of worship, that they maintain the principles

it is affectionately cherished by the congregations, who could scarcely be persuaded to become accustomed to the coldness, and formality, and incoherency, affording little food for the heart, that so often characterizes a service without a fixed order."[50]

Ritualism—an extreme ceremonial, a meaningless repetition of rites, an introduction of such Romish usages as were rejected at the Reformation—is unknown in the Lutheran Church. Even in those countries where an Episcopal Constitution and the greatest correspondence with Mediaeval usages prevails, as in Scandinavia, Lutheran Worship has always retained a pure and high spirituality. Thus writes a careful observer and traveler of large experience: "Here' we find universally prevalent a very "High Church Lutheranism" which many of us have been educated to regard as "Ritualism"—mere dead "Formalism." Be that as it may, I must confess that this very "High Church Lutheranism" with its high Ritual, throughout has produced the highest expression of applied Christianity among the Norwegians, the world has yet seen. There the system has had a most thorough trial for 350 years, and the results, if they prove anything, prove that it most likely promotes the highest gospel graces in heart and life, for here we find the highest type of Christian nation in the world." [51] Such is the conclusive answer Lutherans can make if ever the groundless charge of "High Church" and "Ritualism," is made. "By their fruits shall ye know them" (Matt. vii, 16).

---

embodied in the Augsburg Confession, namely, that unity of doctrine and the administration of the sacraments are sufficient for the true unity of the Church, that differences in rites and ceremonies are not injurious to this unity, that ordinances of men ought not to be forced on the congregations. At the same time it is believed that harmony and edification are secured by pure and holy worship that is common and universal.

[50] Distinctive Doctrines and Usages of the General Bodies of the Lutheran Church, p. n6

[51] M. W. Hamma, D.D.

Luther saw the value of a Common Liturgical Order of Worship. Accordingly, when he published his German Order of Service in 1526 he thus advised: "It would be beautiful and admirable, if in every territory, the order of service would be the same, and the surrounding towns and villages would follow the same." The Patriarch Muhlenberg saw the same need and wrote in 1783 in the closing days of his life: "It would be a most desirable and advantageous thing if all the Evangelical Lutheran congregations in the North American States were united with one another, and if they all used the same order of service and the same hymn-book!" And sagacious observers see and feel that this is one of the greatest needs of American Lutheranism now. Thus Prof. M. Valentine, D.D. says: "A general uniformity is felt to be desirable, but not held to be necessary."[52] Rev. J. G. Butler, D.D. writes: "Greater uniformity in our Church services would conduce greatly to the outer and inner unity of the Church, in which there is now too much that is loose, and in many cases, even disorderly. This uniformity secured in our Churches, the Lutheran Church, which is one Church, would preserve and strengthen the bonds which, under God, I trust will ever make us an undivided and united family of the great household of faith." And that veteran of American Lutheranism, Rev. F. W. Conrad, D.D., Editor of the Lutheran Observer, gives this wise counsel: "This state of nonconformity was the legitimate outgrowth of the principle of freedom in worship maintained by Luther, which, notwithstanding his solemn warning against its perversion, and his emphatic testimony to the desirableness of a uniform church service in all the congregations of a country, was carried to an unwarranted extreme. The same abuse of liberty in worship, and disregard of the importance of uniformity in church services in Germany, have produced the same variety and indifference to uniformity in worship in the Lutheran Churches of America." And writes the Doctor: "A

---

[52] Distinctive Doctrines and Usages of the General Bodies of the Evangelical Lutheran Church, p. 48.

general desire is felt that a uniform Order of Worship may yet be adopted in all the Lutheran Churches of America."[53]

To remedy these evils the General Synod South at Staunton, Virginia, 1876,[54] adopted this resolution: "Resolved, that with a view to promote uniformity in worship and strengthen the bonds of unity throughout all our churches, the Committee on the Revision of the Book of Worship be instructed to confer with the Lutheran General Synod of the United States, and with the Lutheran General Council in America, in regard to the feasibility of adopting but one book containing the same hymns and the same order of service and liturgic forms to be used in all the English-speaking Evangelical Lutheran Churches in the United States." To this proposition the General Synod responded with enthusiasm at its session in Springfield, Ohio, in 1883, where feeling that the movement was Providential, unanimously and with a rising vote, it resolved "that we hail as one of the most auspicious outlooks of our Church in America the prospect of securing a Common Service for all English-speaking Lutherans!" And the General Council having joined these two General Bodies in the movement on "the generic and well-defined basis of the common consent of the pure Lutheran Liturgies of the Sixteenth Century," there resulted what is now known as "The Common Service."

Of the intrinsic merit of this Service Dr. Conrad says: "In the number, variety, and devotional style of its parts, and in beauty and force of expression, the order of worship may justly be regarded as the highest product of the intelligence, piety, culture and taste, guided by the devotional spirit, of the Church of Christ; and is worthy of the respect, not only of every Lutheran, but of every Protestant, and deserves a sincere and fair trial by the pastors and congregations of the three bodies for whom it was prepared."[55]

[53] Luther Memorial Tract, p. 6.—F. W. Conrad, U.U.

[54] On motion of the author, then a pastor at Savannah, Ga.

[55] Lutheran Observer, Oct. 19 and 26, 1888.

Of it, further, a Lutheran can say with pride that it is the order virtually in use by fifty millions of Christians in all quarters of the globe, and therefore of incalculably greater historic and devotional interest than any other book of worship in the world. In harmony with Lutheran principles its use is not made "obligatory upon congregations," or imposed as a law to bind the conscience. It is simply "commended" by the General Bodies, "as serving to edification," and as tending to foster devotion, cement unity, and promote denominational efficiency. As an illustration of the benefits of its use, the Rev. E. T. Horn, D.D., President of the United Synod in the South, says of its introduction there: "It gives order to our worship, secures uniformity among us, provides a system of devotion in harmony with our faith, maintains among us the fundamental doctrines of God's Word and an administration of the Sacraments according to the Gospel, and stores in the minds of our children the form of sound words; and while we rejoice in our accord with the fathers of our own Church and with the Church of all ages, in the use of these venerable forms, the Southern Church has hoped to fulfill her own special vocation in uniting in this the Churches of the General Synod and those of the General Council with her own. This hope seems destined to fulfillment; and already the English Churches of the Synod of Missouri and of the Joint Synod of Ohio are adopting this Common Service of the Lutheran Church."—Distinctive Doctrines and Usages of the General Bodies of the Evangelical Lutheran Church, p. 190.

During the earlier history of America, the Puritanic ideas of worship generally prevalent, were anything but favorable to the popularity of the Lutheran service. But the progress of the country in culture, and in just conceptions of worship, and the marked tendency in all denominations to liturgical services, are drawing special attention to the Lutheran Worship. And its scripturalness, devotional spirit, symmetry, mode, ration, and reproduction of the pure primitive Church Services, are securing it most favorable recognition. This tendency finds notable expression in the great History of the Christian Church, now being issued by Dr. Schaff, where he thus contrasts the Lutheran with other modes of worship: "The Zwinglian and Calvinistic worship depends for its effect too much upon the intellectual and spiritual power of the minister, who can make it either very solemn and impressive, or very cold and barren." "Luther [on the other hand,] who was a poet and a musician, left larger scope for the aesthetic and artistic element; and his Church has developed a rich liturgical literature!" "The Lutheran Church is conservative and liturgical. She retained from the traditional usage what was not inconsistent with evangelical doctrine, while the Reformed Churches of the Zwinglian type aimed at the greatest simplicity!"

It is thus evident that the more Reformed scholars and worshipers compare the barren meagerness of their services with the Lutheran, the more will the contrast of the spiritual beauty and fullness of the latter impress them. It is pleasing to know that Lutheran Worship, after having stood the test of three and a half centuries, is thus in full keeping with the trend of modern liturgical ideas. Thus is the good ever at once both old and new. It is a remark not infrequently made that the Lutheran Service is very like the Episcopalian.

Such a remark results from a want of correct historical information. That there is a general similarity in the worship of these two liturgical Churches is very true. But the similitude is the other way. That is, it is the Episcopal Service which is like the Lutheran. The original Lutheran Service dates from 1523, whereas the Book of Common Prayer only dates from 1549. And just as the English Bible is traceable to German soil and Lutheran influences, and as the Thirty Nine Articles of the Church of England were derived from the fountain head of the Lutheran Augsburg Confession, so the ritual and worship of the Episcopal Church are mainly tributary to, and modelled after the Lutheran liturgies. The principal one of these was the Cologne Liturgy, which the Archbishop of Cologne, who had become a convert to Lutheranism, had Bucer and Melanchthon draw up for him in 1543. Dr. Jacobs in his "Lutheran Movement in England" shows with exhaustive scholarship how in the Church of England the order of Morning and Evening Service, the Litany, the Communion Service, the orders for Baptism, Confirmation, Marriage, Burial, etc. follow more or less closely the Lutheran Orders, often taking leading forms from Luther's identical words. The correspondence of the worship of these two great historic Churches is matter of congratulation to both. But, when it comes to the point as to which one the credit of originating these services is due, historic justice should always be done. The Church of England is the daughter of the Church of Luther. And the daughter has wisely decked herself very largely in the beautiful robes of her spiritual mother.

CHAPTER XI.
RITES AND FESTIVALS IN THE LUTHERAN CHURCH.

"THE Lutheran made no pretext to be a new Church, as if Christ's Church had been totally destroyed, and no Christian Church was existing on the earth. But she claimed to be the old true historic Church purified, reformed, and renewed. No historic chain was therefore to be broken, no rite abolished, no usage abandoned, which was rightfully observed in the ancient Church. Thus says the Augsburg Confession: Art. XV: "Concerning ecclesiastical rites our Churches teach that those rites are to be observed, which may be observed without sin, and are profitable for tranquillity and good order in the Church"— Art. XXVI: "Among us, in large part, the ancient rites are diligently observed. For it is a calumnious falsehood, that all the ceremonies, all the things instituted of old are abolished in our Churches." Apology Of Melanchthon, Chap. IV; "It is pleasing to us that, for the sake of unity and good order Universal Rites Be Observed." That is, usages and forms of worship observed of old and everywhere by Christians, were hallowed by such use, and to be maintained as a bond of unity. The Church historian, Guericke, therefore says: "The Evangelical Lutheran Church retains every undoubtedly ancient festival. In so doing, however, the Lutheran Church reduces them all to their proper significance. The ultra-reformers, on the other hand, by their abrogation of all such commemorations have cut away from beneath their feet the true foundations of history and antiquity."[56]

---

[56] Christian Antiquities p. 197.

The idea of Luther and the Lutheran Church in retaining usages and rites practiced by the universal Christian Church from the time of Christ and the Apostles was to perpetuate a bond of visible unity between all believers. If divisions and discords sadden and disturb us, how agreements and concords that have outlived all differences bridge this chasm of estrangement, and attest that the disciples of Jesus of whatever land, and time, and name, are still one in the bonds of a blessed unity! Another precious feature of the perpetuation of universal usages is the assurance and reverence that come from such ancient and common observance. While the customs of society and civil government are ever subject to change and vacillation, as being but human, how fitting that that kingdom, which is of the Lord Jesus Christ, should be "the same yesterday, today, and forever." In this invariability of customs the believer and even the world find a powerful confirmation of the immutability of the truth and faith of which they are the visible expression. With the Lutheran, that the Romish Church uses a universal rite is no more objection to it, than the use of the Apostles' Creed by that Church is an objection to that venerable symbol. And the non-Lutheran Churches, in disusing universal rites, have in deference alone to groundless prejudice, cast away some of the choicest treasures, and the most potent and beneficent influences of the Christian Church.

In illustration of these principles, the Lutheran Church observed the Christian Year. While many Saints' and Martyrs' days and excesses were stripped from it, the Chief Festivals, those "wreaths about the pillars of the Christian Year" were retained. This was in keeping with Luther's advice: "Especially should all keep Christmas, Circumcision, Epiphany, the Easter Festival, Ascension, and Pentecost—unchristian legends and songs having been done away." [57] While thus the Lutheran Church rejected the Romish pseudo-festivals, and abolished the great mass of Saints' days, she by no means, however, set aside the memorial days of the Apostles, St. Stephen, the Martyr. But she retained these as being "an example of

[57] The Christian Year Horn, p. 53.

the believers," in Christian heroism, and godly virtues and graces. Accordingly, Luther said that there could be no better spiritual discipline for Christian youth than to place in their hands brief lives of the apostles, martyrs, and saints, discarding any legendary and superstitious features. Dr. Seiss fitly says of the Lectionary for these Minor Festivals which our Church has appointed, that "it is particularly valuable for a complete rounding out of the system that prevails in the arrangement of the Pericopes for the Christian Church Year. These selections conduct us into quite a different field from that of the other festivals. They bring into greater prominence the element of biography and personal character and experience. They show us more of applied Christianity."[58] And of the rare spiritual value of their treatment in the pulpit his late noble volume is a worthy illustration.

The Christian Year revolves about Jesus Christ as its center, and its purpose is to show forth the successive stages of His life, and to interpret these for the edification of the believer's spiritual life. "The Year of the Ancient Church had for its foundations the great facts of the life of our Lord. All stress is laid upon the Word; no sanctity belongs to the day. The Lutheran Church, therefore, restored the Church Year to its purity."[59] And Ahlfeld beautifully says: "As the earth moves around the visible sun, so the Church moves around the sun of divine grace— so she travels through the sacred history of the Savior. Her spring is the lovely season of Christmas and Epiphany, when Christ is born. Her summer is the season of Lent and the passion time of Jesus Christ. And her harvest and autumn are the Whitsuntide days, when the Holy Spirit is poured out upon the disciples, and when, in the long, lovely Trinity Sundays, one kind after another of the gifts of the Triune God is borne into the granary of the heart."

[58] Lectures on the Gospel and Epistles for the Minor Festivals, p. 4.

[59] The Christian Year, Horn, p, 53.

On Advent Sunday, therefore, the Lutheran Church begins the Christian Year, and calls upon all her members to make a holy beginning in piety and Christian activity. On Christmas Day, with joy and thanksgiving, all gather about the holy child Jesus in the sanctuary. On Palm Sunday, the catechumens are presented to the Lord. On Easter, the Churches resound with the mighty rapture of the Resurrection. And so to the end. On all the Sundays the Lessons— the Epistle and Gospel for the day—are read; those selections of Scripture which have the sanction of the usage of more than a thousand years. To the chief ancient festivals the Lutheran Church has added another, that of the Reformation. This is observed on the 31st of October, the anniversary of the beginning of the blessed work of the Reformation by Luther nailing up the famous theses.

This observance of the Christian Year by the Lutheran Church, exempted from all Romish and ritualistic obligatory fasts and practices, not only is entirely without objection, but is eminently conducive to the production of a sound, rotund, conservative, spiritual life. With regard to objections urged against its observance, the Lutheran Review makes this forcible reply: "What a wealth of holy memories and sacred associations cluster around the festivals of the Church Year to those who are accustomed to observe them. How lost we would feel and how we should miss these festivals if they were suddenly stricken from the calendar. And yet the non-liturgical churches ignore the Church Year altogether, because they are afraid it savors of popery, and because these festivals are not commanded to be observed by the Word of God. We can only pity their childish fears, while we must protest against their inconsistencies. They reject the Church Year, which is observed by the vast majority of Christendom, on the plea that the Bible does not enjoin it, while at the same time they institute a Week of Prayer in January of each year. But where is the warrant for such a Week of Prayer? The zeal of would-be reformers very often gets the better of their discretion, as is abundantly evident in the Puritanic obliteration of all the Church festivals."[60] The following notable utterance of the extremely Broad Church and liberalistic Phillips Brooks, shows how utterly groundless and unreasonable is the prejudice entertained by some even among us, as if an observance of the Pericope of the Gospel and Epistles was infected with ritualism. He says: "Look at the way the pulpit teaches. I venture to say that there is nothing so unreasonable in any other branch of teaching. You are a minister, and you are to instruct these people in the truths of God, to bring God's message to them. All the vast range of God's revelation and of man's duty is open to you. And how do you proceed? If you are like most ministers there is no order, no progress, no consecutive purpose, in your teaching. You never begin at the beginning and proceed step by step to the end of any course of orderly instruction. No other instruction ever was given so. No hearer has the least idea, as he goes to your Church, what you will preach to him about that day. It is hopeless to him to try to get ready for your teaching. It is this observance of the Church Year to which we owe so much as a help to the orderliness of our preaching. It still leaves largest liberty. It is no bondage within which any man is hampered. But the great procession of the year, sacred to our best human instincts, with the accumulated reverence of ages, leads those who walk in it, at least once every year, past all the great Christian facts, and however careless and selfish be the preacher, will not leave it in his power to keep them from his people. The Church Year, too, preserves the personality of our religion. It is concrete and picturesque. The historical Jesus is forever there. It lays each life continually down beside the perfect life, that it may see at once its imperfection and its hope."[61]

The beautiful rite of Confirmation is retained in the Lutheran Church. In the primitive Church this was originally administered by the officiating minister as the closing ceremonial of Baptism, in imitation of the apostolic practice, (Acts 19:6). In the course of time

[60] New York: E. F. Eilert, Editor.

[61] Lectures on Preaching, pp. 90-91.

it came to be administered by the bishop alone as in the Romish and Episcopal Churches. The Lutheran Church has returned to the primitive usage of its administration by each pastor. "Its idea of confirmation is that of a renewal of the baptismal covenant, a conscious and responsible assumption by the individual himself, of the vow, which at his baptism, had been made for him by his sponsors. Its principal features are the catechetical exercises, the confession, and the vow, and its purpose a new-kindled devotion."[62] Beyond doubt the majority of Protestant Churches have made a great mistake and experience a yet greater loss in their rejection of this ancient, beautiful, and useful ceremony of Confirmation, as a means of introducing especially the baptized youth into the privileges and duties of public Church-membership.

The rite of Confession, as a fit preparatory discipline for the reception of the Lord's Supper, is universally practiced in Lutheran Churches. It is based on the words of Jesus to His disciples: "Receive the Holy Ghost. Whosoever sins you remit, they are remitted unto them; and whosoever sins you retain, they are retained" (Jn. xx, 22-23); and upon the custom of the Ancient Church. Luther protested against the Romish perversion of the words of Christ, as shown in the practice of Auricular Confession. He taught that the "Power of the Keys," i.e., the absolution from sins was not absolute, but only exhibitory, and was not limited to a priestly order, but a prerogative of the universal priesthood. He objected also to confession as obligatory, and to the necessity of an enumeration of all sins. With these limitations, however, Luther placed a very high estimate on the disciplinary value of Confession. He therefore makes use of this definition in the small catechism: "Confession consists of two parts; the one is, that we confess our sins; the other, that we receive absolution or forgiveness through the pastor as of God himself, in no wise doubting, but firmly believing that our sins are thus forgiven before God in heaven." "The views of Luther on Confession were expressed by Melanchthon in the Augsburg Confession, and adopted

---

[62] Schaff-Herzog Encyclopedia, Vol. I, p. 530.

by the Lutheran Church, which at the same time so changed the character of Private Confession as to divest it of its unscriptural features. It was not imposed upon the consciences of the people as necessary to obtain justification, but rather extended to them as a privilege. An opportunity was thereby afforded to every member who had any trouble on his mind concerning his sins to reveal the matter to his pastor, in order to receive instruction and comfort. And the subject was thus removed from the sphere of ministerial authority to that of the pastoral care of souls, in verification of which Melanchthon explains Private Absolution as retained in the Churches, as nothing more than "the true voice of the Gospel" addressed to penitent souls by the ministers of Christ."[63]

The exercise of the rite of Confession in this pure Scriptural sense was distinctive of the Lutheran, as over against the other Protestant Churches at the time of the Reformation, and has continued so to the present time. "It was left to the great revival of apostolical christianity in the 16th century to clear away the rubbish that had accumulated around this institution. Zwingli utterly repudiated the traditional Power of the Keys, and confined it to the social sphere of the Church, the power of admitting and excluding members. Calvin held the same view except that he also included preaching. The Lutheran theologians, on the other hand, while retaining the old forms, gave to them, as it were, a regeneration. To them, absolution was nothing less than the Word of God which must be believed as truly, as if it were a voice from heaven. Ordinarily it was pronounced by the minister, not as a priestly mediator, but as a minister of the Church, deriving his authority from Christ indirectly through the Church."[64] Luther, with his intense religious and churchly feelings deemed confession invaluable to his spiritual experience. He says: "Not for the treasures of the whole world would I give up the privilege of private confession, for I know what strength

---

[63] Rev. F. W. Conrad, D.D., on Luther's Smaller Catechism, p. 146.

[64] Rev. G. U. Wenner, D.D., on The Power of the Keys.

and comfort I have derived from it. Nobody knows what it can do, until he has fought and contended with the devil. I would long since have been overcome and destroyed, if this confession had not sustained me/' In the general practice of the Lutheran Church the Confession of Sins is not private, [which is reserved for exceptional cases] but public. It is regarded as a most salutary preparation for the reception of the Lord's Supper, which no one should fail to observe, unless prevented by necessity. Next to the Holy Sacrament itself, the devout Lutheran prizes the opportunity to make public confession before the Church, and to receive that declaration of Absolution which the official representative of the Church is authorized to declare to the true penitent.

CHAPTER XII.
THE LUTHERAN AN ORTHODOX CHURCH.

CHRISTIANITY in our time has come upon an extraordinary phenomenon—the glorification of Heresy. The primary characteristic of a Christian is Faith. Christians, therefore, have from the first worn the distinctive title: believers. Credo —I believe—begins the Apostles Creed. Christians by no means forego reason, but they do feel with Thomas a Kempis, that "Human reason is feeble and may be deceived: but true faith cannot be deceived."[65] It was in this profound spiritual sense that Augustine wrote: "Faith makes Christians: Reason makes heretics." If there was any deadly sin from which the saints of old shrank it was heresy—the denial, perversion, or commingling with error of the true Christian faith, delivered by the Lord Jesus Christ and his Holy Apostles. Consequently St. Paul warns Christians: "A man that is an heretic, after the first and second admonition reject" (Tit. iii; 9.); meaning that this is an evil that dare not be temporized with, even as a viper dare not be taken to the bosom, or a traitor admitted within the camp. And St. Peter cautions us to be on vigilant watch against those "who secretly bring damnable heresies" (2 Pet. 2:1), lest thereby the Christian citadel be undermined.

As an illustration of the feeling of the primitive Christians oh this point, Eusebius, the early Church historian, records the tradition received from Polycarp, the martyr, that on one occasion the apostle John entered one of the ancient baths, but finding that the heresiarch Cerinthus was in one of the adjoining rooms, he hastily fled from the place, saying: "Let us flee, lest the bath fall in, as long as Cerinthus,

[65] Book IV: Chap. XVIII.

the enemy of the truth, is within." [66] The source of this strong aversion was that "the truth as it is in Jesus" is the most priceless treasure of Christianity; and, that even a more deadly enemy of it than the avowed infidel is he who, while falsely professing to be a Christian, uses this profession as a vantage ground to "secretly bring in damnable heresies."

But what a contrast to this holy sensitiveness do we see at the present juncture. Heresies are multiplying on every hand. Heresies, too, not as mild and comparatively as non-essential as that of Cerinthus. But heresies of the destructive and deadly kind. It is claimed that a majority of the books of the Bible, instead of being written by their professed and inspired authors, are literary forgeries of quite other ages. The Bible is held no longer to be an infallible book, but full of discrepancies and errors which were also in the original text. Christ himself is declared to have been fettered by many limitations, which led him into incorrect statements respecting the authorship of these books. Kuenen, Wellhausen, Driver, Briggs, etc., know a great deal more about them than He did, though He lived 1900 years nearer their origin and had the not inconsiderable advantage of being Divine. In fact the whole origin of the Bible is treated as natural, like that of any other book. "We are at length beginning to realize the gravity of the present state of the Old Testament controversy. The Traditional views are being examined under the light of modern discoveries, and efforts are beginning to be made fairly to put in contrast that inspired and trustworthy record of the past, bearing the name of the Old Testament, and sealed with a belief of more than two thousand years in its genuineness and integrity, with that strange conglomerate of myth, legend, fabrication, idealized narrative, falsified history, dramatized fable, and after-event prophecy, to which modern critical analysis has sought to reduce that which the Church, day by day, calls the most Holy Word of Almighty God." [67]

[66] Ecclesiastical History, chap. XXVIII.

[67] Christus Comprobator—Bishop Ellicott, p. 93.

The same heretical treatment is applied to the Christian doctrines. The divinity of Jesus is sought to be abolished from the creed. The vicarious atonement of our Lord, is reduced to a mere salutary example of suffering. Salvation by faith is denied. It does not matter what one believes. Jew, Infidel, Pagan, and Christian alike, will be asked how they have lived, not what they have believed. Hence the venerable Christian creeds are denounced as yokes of tyranny. The sacraments are held to be of inconsiderable moment. The resurrection is ridiculed as a scientific impossibility and absurdity. And so on through the list. Now, it is perfectly evident that these heresies invalidate the whole Christian structure. They leave no authentic Bible; no veritable Christ; no fatal sin; no true atonement; no real Church; no historical Christianity; no visible Kingdom of God. Their triumph means the disappearance of Christianity in its visible, historic form from the earth. Now it is nothing new for Christianity to be assailed by heresies. Ever has the banner of truth had to battle its way against bitter foes. But what is new and unparalleled is that these heresies are sought to be legitimized. Their advocates are not to be censured or excommunicated, but to be extolled. The journal of a leading religious denomination thus writes: "Orthodoxy is stagnation and spiritual death." "The heretics of to-day are the Christian leaders of to-morrow." Those who have denied the divinity of Christ, as Martineau, "are the High Priests and Prophets of mankind," writes a Professor in regular standing in Union Theological Seminary, New York. How closely akin are these utterances to that of the infidel Ingersoll, who cries: "Orthodoxy is retrogression and tyranny—Heresy is the eternal dawn." In fact, in many religious quarters, there is no surer road to popularity than to pose as a heretic. One has but bitterly to assail some great Christian doctrine, and he is heralded as a scholar, a champion of progress and freedom, a remonstrant against effete dogmas, and his fame travels beyond the seas. To such an extent has this gone that the late Spurgeon felt himself compelled to retire from fellowship with the

Baptist union in England, and after the recent failure of the attempt to convict the most daring leader of the destructive critical school in America a noted infidel said: "Old John Knox and Calvin must have turned in their graves, when it was decided by the Presbyterian Church that this man was right.[68] Why, do you know that in a little while the Protestant Churches will be waiting to take me in!" And while this exaggeration was in keeping with the orator's ribald style, yet his and his hearers elation were significant of the radical trend of much of modern Protestantism.

But amid this wild onset and uproar of heresy, the Lutheran Church stands firm. She abides immovably grounded on the truth. Under her feet is the Rock of Ages, and the waves of hell shall not prevail against her. She is not compelled to any creed revision. She does not canonize heretics. She is not embarrassed by heresy trials. She does not abridge a hair's breadth her acceptance of the Bible. She does not stumble at holy mysteries, but holds, as even the great critic Lessing admits: ".For what sort of a Revelation would that be which reveals nothing?" She compromises not a single doctrine. She stands where Christ stood; where the apostles stood; where the primitive Christian stood; where the true confessors all through the Mediaeval darkness stood; where Luther and the Reformers stood, when they emerged into the light; and where the saints of all ages have stood; and where by God's grace she will stand to the end of time. She unreservedly accepts and holds to the three Ecumenical (universal) Creeds—the Apostles, the Nicene, and the Athanasian. And she holds to the unaltered Augsburg Confession. These she does not hold as the Bible, but as correct witnesses to the faith of the Bible. Thus she voices her belief with that of the current Christendom of all the centuries. She lifts up her testimony in sweet and unbroken accord with the universal "communion of saints." She is not a heretical, but an orthodox Church. She does not glory in error, but in truth. She does not lift her sword to assail Christianity, but to defend

---

[68] To the credit of this great Church, this action was reversed by the General Assembly at Washington.

it. These eloquent words, lately spoken, correctly define the Lutheran position: "Cling to the old faith. There is much falling away on this point. People are too fondly persuading themselves that the Creeds which cheered and sustained so many generations must now be expurgated or damned. The world is thronged with zealots, busy building straw bridges between the orthodoxy of ages and the unbeliefs and shallow self-assertions of this arrogant and self-lauding generation. The greatest need of our times is the re-Christening of Christendom. A flabby goodishness, which makes nothing of doctrine, Church and Sacraments, is not Christianity, and only deceives those who trust to it. What men need is positive truth —a teaching that has back-bone in it, and stands out solid and erect above the muddy sentimentalities of the day—a teaching which anxious and perishing souls can lay hold on and feel that they have something substantial on which to rest. There is such a thing as clear and positive truth. God's word presents it. Christ embodied it. Prophets and Apostles preached it. It has been echoed down through the centuries. Our sainted Confessors revoiced it in our immortal Augustana.

While thus refusing to place natural reason above Faith, the Lutheran Church takes care not to divorce Faith from Good Works. She "discountenances all dead orthodoxy, and next to purity of doctrine lays all stress upon showing the faith in a Christian life. She has from the beginning tried to enforce strict Church discipline in her congregations, and requires of those who seek to be admitted to membership evidence of a Christian life. In all relations of Christian and Church life she urges the necessity of showing the true faith in good works."[69] As the truth of God is the seed of spiritual life, so she holds that the purer the orthodoxy, the better and richer the harvest of practical godliness.

This is the unique attitude of the Lutheran Church, that she stands to-day the one solidly unswerving witness of God on earth to the unimpaired "faith which was once delivered unto the saints"

---

[69] Distinctive Doctrines and Usages of the Lutheran Church, p.67.

(Jude 3). Rationalism, the guise under which this heretical inundation is now threatening Christendom, has ever been alien to the spirit of the Lutheran Church. Bahrdt, the father of the modern school of rationalists, discerningly remarked: "That in the doctrine of the Lord's Supper I was more Reformed than Lutheran, will be supposed as a matter of course."[70] And though Germany, because of its brilliant mental culture, is the nursery of Rationalism, yet it is not found in the Lutheran Church. Its home is in the universities, and in the schools of Reformed theology. And what is often overlooked is, that similarly the most powerful and numerous defenses of evangelical Christianity come from Germany—from its great Evangelical Lutheran scholars.

Prof. Christlieb some time since wrote the Homiletic Monthly: "This sketch shows that the overwhelming majority of the German ministers of to-day are positively Evangelical; and at the same time that the overwhelming majority of them are more or less positively Lutheran." The widow of the late evangelical scholar, Dr. Howard Crosby, has just been visiting Germany, and this is her testimony from a non-Lutheran standpoint: "We have been most agreeably surprised by the spiritual preaching we have heard everywhere in Germany; not a word of poor, finite Rationalism, as we had feared, but simple faith in original form, with a rich armory of Bible texts, making one feel that the only real strength comes from Scripture knowledge brought to remembrance by the Holy Spirit."[71] So writes also an observing Lutheran layman, "J. A. B.," in a late number of "The Lutheran World:" "I am in Prussia and in the capital of the German Empire, and, after spending six months in the Land of Luther's Church, I say that the members of the Church which bears his name in America, can look across the ocean for an example of Church love and fidelity. Lutherans of the United States do not be deceived by what you hear of the tendency to "Briggsism" among the

---

[70] German Protestantism, Kahnis, p. 136.

[71] New York Observer, September 18, 1892.

Germans. The clergymen, as a class, are holy, earnest men of God, preaching the gospel of Jesus Christ, and working for the salvation of souls. As for the people, the plain people, with the exception of a small number of the various "free thinkers," they know of no disputes as to the Confession nor of any dogma of the Church. Every person, of the age of fourteen and over, is the owner of a hymn-book which contains the Augsburg Confession. It and the Bible settle the whole matter."

The same is notably true of Lutheran pulpits in the United States. However uncertain one may feel as to whether orthodoxy will confirm his faith, or dangerous heresies offend his ear, on entering other Protestant Churches, we do not believe there is a Lutheran pulpit in all this land from which one will not hear the simple, pure, old gospel. Accordingly, President Patton of Princeton, recently remarked to the author that one of the most auspicious signs for Christendom was the unswerving fidelity of Lutheran pastors throughout the entire world to unimpaired Christian truth.

The Lutheran Is An Orthodox Church. This is her distinctive, her unique, her unrivalled glory. She is "the Church of the pure doctrine."[72] With her, orders, polity, methods, forms, are as nothing, the faith is all in all. Like the Church in Philadelphia spoken of in the Apocalypse, amid all the alluring degeneracies of these modern times, she "has kept My word, and has not denied My name." And therefore does .' He who walks in the midst of the seven golden candlesticks," say to her: "I also will keep you from the hour of temptation, which shall come upon all the world, to try them that dwell upon the earth. Hold that fast which you have, that no man takes your crown" (Rev. 3:8, 9.).

---

[72] Church History, Kurtz, Vol. Ill, p. 39.

CHAPTER XIII.
LUTHERANS AND THE CHURCH.

LUTHERANS believe not only in Christianity but in the Church. They hold that the spiritual life exists in and through a visible form, "Christ's body, which is the Church" (Col. 1:24). Piety has an historical as well as a spiritual side. A Lutheran, therefore, does not regard as either Scriptural or safe that Christianity which is indifferent to and independent of churchliness.

The Lutheran conception of the Church, first, is that it is divine. It is "the household of God —built upon the foundation of the apostles and prophets, Jesus Christ himself being the chief corner-stone" (Ephes. 2:20). It is the congregation of the saints—all those who are joined by faith to the Lord Jesus Christ. Its purpose is the preaching of the Word and the celebration of the Sacraments, for the conversion of sinners, and the edification of the faithful. Jesus Christ is the "Head of the Church," and its members are one in Him, and by this means are one with one another. "This communion we then call holy, because in it the Holy Ghost is operating, to sanctify it; catholic, because however widely the members of the Church are scattered, yet at all times and in all places the same faith is confessed; apostolic, because its faith resting upon that proclaimed by the apostles, has never, in the course of time been changed."[73]

The Church, as thus divine, is entirely unique, and is not to be compared with any merely human society or institution. But it is separated from these by an impassable chasm of superiority. Its obligations, its claims, its powers, proceed from God, and are endued

---

[73] Lutheran Doctrinal Theology—Schmid, p. 599.

with the might of the Holy Ghost. The Church is the "Body of Christ," the organ by which He continuously lives and mightily works on the earth. This clothes it with supernatural spiritual forces, such as pertain to ho merely natural or moral association whatever.

The Church is visible and invisible. By the visible Church we mean the Church in that broader sense in which it comprises all those who, by observance of the outward conditions, are regular members of the Church. But by the invisible Church we mean the Church in that narrower sense in which it comprises alone the truly regenerate, those whose inner union with Christ complies with their outward profession of Him. But the Lutheran Church repudiates such a perversion of the idea of the invisible Church, as would make it embrace those who reject Christ's visible terms of communion. "Nor is the Church of the elect said to be invisible because the pious and elect have no intercourse whatever with the visible ministry of the Word and Sacraments, and with the outward practice of divine worship."[74] The invisible Church is not larger and more extensive, than the visible, but just the reverse. Nor is it apart from the visible, but in and a part of it. "The relation between them is this, that the Church in the narrower sense exists in the midst of the Church in the wider sense."[75] "The Church invisible becomes visible through the Word and Sacraments."[76] One may be in the visible Church, and yet not be in the invisible. But the divine order is that one cannot be in the invisible Church without being in the visible. Here the rule is, subject to such exceptions as God in His wisdom and mercy may allow, that laid down by St. Augustine: "He who has not the Church for his Mother cannot have God for his Father."

Lutherans further hold the Church to be one, "There is one Lord, one faith, one baptism" (Ephes. 4:5). "And there shall be one

---

[74] Gerhard XI ; 83.

[75] Lutheran Doctrinal Theology—Schmid, p. 600.

[76] Holman Lecture on the Church, P. Bergstresser, D.D.

fold, and one Shepherd" (John 10:16). Diverse Churches with differing faiths and antagonistic confessions—the one a protest against the other, the one unchurching the other—are not the idea of the gospel. Such separated and rival organizations do not hold the relation to each other of branches of the Vine, limbs of the Body, or natural members of the Christian Family. Hence the Lutheran Church aspires after a true Christian unity, an oneness in "the truth as it is in Jesus." And assured that she holds that faith, and administers the sacraments in their purity, while not denying that others are more or less true Churches, or contain regenerated souls, yet she aims to bring back to the pure confession of the truth, all such as have more or less erred therefrom, and thus to realize on earth the "one holy Catholic and Apostolic Church," confessed in the Nicene Creed.

The Church, further, is the divine instrumentality for salvation. To it are committed the Word and Sacraments, the Means of Grace. As these are the divinely ordained agencies for causing justifying faith, men must come to these ordinances for salvation: "For the obtaining of faith, the ministry of teaching the Gospel, and administering the Sacraments was instituted. For by the Word and Sacraments, as by instruments, the Holy Spirit is given." Augsburg Confession, Art. V. For the administration of these Means of Grace, there must be a ministry. Hence results the Ministerial Office, and no one has the right to officiate in these holy things, unless he receives a regular call from the Church. The witness and seal of this call is the rite of ordination.

As to the Church have been committed these divine powers, agencies, and instrumentalities of grace and salvation, to her belongs the regeneration of society. Her spiritual forces alone are competent to the overthrow of moral evil. She alone can successfully cope with impiety, immorality, and vice. Where all human societies are impotent, and where all reforms undertaken on a merely moral basis will fail, she can perform moral wonders in the name of Christ "working with her, and confirming the Word by signs following" (Mark 16:20). All great movements then of a reformatory character, every attempt at the moral regeneration of society, and all uplifting power for the rescue and redemption of mankind, must issue from the Church, and be conducted under her guidance. Here she is at war with many of the skeptical theories promulgated by social reformers of our time.

To the Church exercised through the ministerial office, pertains the Power of the Keys. This the Augsburg Confession, Article XXVIII, thus defines: "The Power of the Keys, or the power of the bishops, by the rule of the Gospel, is a power, or commandment from God, of preaching the Gospel, of remitting or retaining sins, and of administering the Sacraments. For Christ doth send His Apostles with the charger "As the Father has sent me, even so send I you. Receive the Holy Ghost; whosoever sins you remit, they are remitted unto them; and whosoever sins you retain, they are retained" (John 20:21-23). Again, [the Power of the Keys is] the jurisdiction to judge in regard to doctrine, and to exclude from the communion of the Church. And herein of necessity the Churches ought by Divine right to render obedience unto them [the bishops or ministers]." That is, to the Church belongs the preservation of the pure gospel. To her, for safe keeping and transmission, are "committed the oracles of God" (Rom. 3:2). She is "the pillar and ground of the truth" (1 Tim. 3:15). In this capacity she has framed the canon of Holy Scripture. She has faithfully kept and transmitted the record of divine revelation. And 'she is the witness-bearing Church, in that by her creeds and confessions she bears unanimous and continuous testimony to the true teaching of this Scripture. The Church thus has a history and is known by historical marks. And the difference between her history and secular histories is that her history directly bears the formative hand of the Holy Ghost, and therefore most markedly reflects the divine guidance. "Howbeit when He, the Spirit of Truth is come, He will guide you into all truth" (John 16:13). As we study the course of the Christian Church through the centuries, we observe the leadings and trace the footprints of the Son of God.

The Church, thus, is an orderly kingdom with a constituted government, so that in it "all things may be done decently and in order" (1 Cor. 14:40). The Church is not destitute of authority. It has the power of self-preservation. There is a legitimate ecclesiastical government. Within due limits there must within the Church, and with regard to its spiritual officers be rule and obedience, as the

Scripture says: "Obey them that have the rule over you, and submit yourselves; for they watch for your souls, as they that must give account" (Heb. 13:17). To this Power of the Keys pertains the exercise of discipline, the excommunication of heretics, that the faith may be kept intact, and the correction or excommunication of the immoral, that the fellowship may be kept pure. And to this authority, legitimately exercised, everyone must bow, even as it is written: "Tell it unto the Church; but if he neglect to hear the Church, let him be unto thee as a heathen man and a publican" (Matt18).

The congregation, however, is the ultimate source of power. As Lutherans hold the universal priesthood of all believers, the ministerial office, and hence "the Power of the Keys," is rooted in the congregation. For the sake of order it simply delegates its rights to some fellow member that he may officiate for all. The Scriptural or New Testament Church was organized by the setting apart of Presbyters or Bishops—synonyms for the one office of Minister—and Deacons; and this system is that of the Lutheran Church. For the sake of order, these Ministers, with lay representatives from the congregations, constitute themselves into synods. As these synods represent the embodied wisdom and piety of the Church, it is the moral duty of the congregations to render obedience to them. The individual congregation is under the government of the Church Council, consisting of the Pastor and Deacons, or Elders, as they are often called. At the head of the congregation stands the Minister, to preach the Gospel, administer the Sacraments, conduct the rites of Confession and Confirmation, execute discipline, and in general to exercise the Power of the Keys. "The pastor, by virtue of his office, is at the head, not only of the Sunday School, but of the Church Council and every organization connected with the Church. The superintendent of the Sunday School, and presidents and officers of the various organizations, are in no respect equal, much less superior, in authority to the pastor. Because of pastoral duties, or various other considerations, he may absent himself from any meeting, or even when he is present, he may leave the meeting entirely in the hands of chosen officers; but the fact remains that the pastor is not only the spiritual leader, but the ordained head of all the affairs of the congregation. We think this position is unquestionably the correct

Scriptural and therefore Lutheran, view of the relation between the pastor and all associations in the congregation."[77]

In Europe much injury has resulted from the union of Church and State in Lutheran countries. This arises from a perversion of the Lutheran theory. The Church and State, as both ordained of God, and necessary to secular and spiritual order, have a vital connection. With the Family, they constitute those three estates or pillars upon which is supported the whole fabric of society. The Church, therefore, should instil loyalty to the State. And the State should render spiritual deference and allegiance to the Church. But when the Church wields force to execute her authority, she transcends her spiritual realm and encroaches upon the prerogatives of the State. And when the State appoints ministers, maintains professors in theological chairs, and decides questions of doctrine, she encroaches upon the Church's legitimate spiritual supremacy, assumes the Power of the Keys, foments confusion, promotes heresy, and causes general disorder.

Such is the Lutheran conception of the Church. It differs radically from the Romish idea in this that it denies that the Church depends upon a certain external constitution or order, but upon the pure confession of the truth. It denies likewise the Papal Primacy, that the Pope is the successor of the Apostle Peter and the infallible Head of the Church. It denies, too, an absolute, instead of a declarative, power upon the part of the priests, as a sacerdotal order, to forgive sins. And it denies also the infallibility of a General Council of the Church, for even this has been known to err. There always remains, as of the very kernel and essence of Protestantism, the exercise of Private Judgment, the right of appeal to the Holy Scripture, as the only supreme, inerrant, infallible, and final tribunal.

This Lutheran view of the Church, likewise, differs from that of the Protestant Episcopal, in that it denies the existence of three orders in the Church, viz. Deacons, Priests, and Bishops—of which three orders there is no account in the Scriptures, while there is

---

[77] Lutheran Observer, Editorial, March 17th, 1893.

positive testimony that there was no such distinction in the apostolic age, or first century of the Church. And it likewise repudiates the claim of the apostolic succession of the Episcopate, and the attempt to invalidate the legitimate ministry of those who have not been Episcopally ordained, and to invalidate the Church membership of such as have not been Episcopally confirmed. This is making the Church to depend upon orders instead of faith, which is contrary to the Scriptures.

The Lutheran view of the Church none the less differs from the Calvinistic and Zwinglian Churches, who, on the other hand, often take too low and latitudinarian views of it. These depreciate the legitimate authority of the Church, virtually nullifying the Power of the Keys, and by dissociating saving grace from the sacraments, and by a false conception of the invisible Church as apart from the visible, deprive the Church of its chief significance as God's ordained kingdom of salvation.

The current views in America, respecting the Church, are to a large degree infected with Rationalism. The prevalent tendency often is to regard the Church as little better than "a purely human organization, very much on a level with other societies."[78] That Christ can be found without the Church, that saving grace may be given through other channels than the Word and Sacraments, that "the Faith once delivered to the saints," is liable to change with each decade like the latest assumption of science, or like the platform of a political convention, are the sentiments most in vogue with the Low or Broad Churchism of the time. What the Christianity of our day then needs is the element of Churchliness. A due regard for the uniqueness of "the Church of God;" a fitting reverence for its sacraments and historic usages; a becoming regard to judicious ecclesiastical authority and order; and a lively appreciation of the necessity and beauty of Churchly graces and virtues.

And herein we see again the great value of the Lutheran view and teaching in regard to the Church. Nothing is more required by

---

[78] The Church, Schaff-Herzog Encyclopedia, Vol. I, p. 474.

the present situation, to correct errors, to restrain false tendencies, and to promote the welfare of Christendom, than insistence upon the Lutheran theory of the Church. So wise, so Scriptural, so Catholic, so intensely Protestant, so guarded, and so important to meet present demands, is her testimony on this point, that every Lutheran should feel it his mission not alone to intelligently understand it, but also to illustrate it in act and in life.

CHAPTER XIV.
LUTHERAN PIETY.

THE doctrinal character of a Church has a direct bearing upon the religious life. Thus the Lutheran or Calvinistic systems produce markedly diverse types of Christians. The deeper, fuller, more childlike faith of the Lutheran results in a deeper, richer spiritual life. His intense hold upon the very heart of the gospel, causes a still inner spirit of unusual beauty, depth, and power. Consequently, sensationalism, turbulent revivalism, and all forms of religious demonstrativeness, are altogether foreign to him. The meditative, devotional, quietistic temper is the characteristic Lutheran one. Still, but. deep; quiet, but mighty; not in name 'but in power. The Lutheran spirit is simple, modest, and unobtrusive. Writes Dr. Schaff: "The Lutheran piety has its peculiar charm, the charm of Mary, who sat at Jesus' feet and heard His word. It has a rich inward life. The Lutheran Church numbers her mystics who bathed in the ocean of infinite love. She has sung the most fervent hymns to the Savior, and holds sweet childlike intercourse with the heavenly Father." This mystical spirit is reflected in her doctrinal literature and prayer books, which are the richest in the world—as Arndt's *True Christianity*, Gerhard's *"Meditationes Sacrae,"* "Gotthold's *Emblems,"* etc.

Another characteristic of Lutheran Piety is its cheerful and hearty joyousness. It is not austere or Puritanical. It is not narrow or one-sided. It has nothing in it of the severity of asceticism. It is not the enforced perfunctory service of the slave, but the free, willing obedience of the son. It enters with a frank and hearty spirit into all the joyousness spread about in the kingdom of nature. Love being its center and keystone, its generalizing influences soften and irradiate the whole Lutheran system. Believing that the good things of life were meant by the Creator to be enjoyed, it does not hold to a theory of abstinence, but "temperate in all things" is its motto. "It excels in honesty, kindness, affection, cheerfulness, and that '*Gemuthlichkeit*' for which other nations have not even a name."[79]

This happy temper is imbibed from its founder. With all Luther's poignant conviction of sin, his life of theological battle, and his superhuman labors, he yet was intensely human, genial, and sympathetic. "With childlike joy he recognized God's gifts in nature, in garden and fields plants and cattle. ' He was enraptured with the beauties of Spring, the bloom of the flowers, and the song of the birds."[80] He loved home, children, friends. In the evening, after his hard studies, he would gather about the social circle with his friends, and dissolve his soul to the melodies of his lute. Thus he touched whole spheres of human nature to which Calvin was a stranger.

And this freedom and sunshine of Luther's nature characterize the piety of Lutheran, as contrasted with Reformed peoples. "The religious life in the Reformed Churches is characterized generally by harsh legalism, rigorous renunciation of the world, coupled with unbending decision and energy of will. It is the spirit of Calvin which impresses on it this character, and determines its doctrine." [81] The contrasted free joyousness, larger Christian liberty, innocent amusements, non-Puritanical conception of the Sabbath, etc. in Lutheran lands, are often misinterpreted and grossly misrepresented by those reared under Calvinistic influences.

A third feature of Lutheran Piety is its practical character. This is shown in the religiousness and Churchliness of popular life, the propagation of Missions, the erection of Orphans' Homes,

---

[79] Dr. John Hall of New York, writes from Germany to the Mail and Express: "There is one feature of German life, as it comes under the notice of a tourist, which deserves commendation— namely, the general sobriety of the people. An intoxicated person is not often seen."

[80] Koestlin's Life of Luther, p. 597.

[81] Kurtz's Church History, Vol. Ill, p. 59.

Deaconesses' Houses, and general beneficent and pious activity. Nowhere in the world is the practical result of Christianity in individual uprightness and household piety so marked as among the Scandinavians, who are almost wholly Lutherans. Says the noted traveler, Du Chaillu: "Passing along their highways, after the lamps are lit, the farmers may be seen with the big Bible on the table, and reading it to the family. Mothers sit by the cradle of their babes and lull them to sleep with hymns and psalms. They say, "We want our children from their birth to hear us sing praises to God; we want them to fear and love God when they grow up, for He is good to us all." "There are tens of thousands of laymen, members of the State Church, earnest Christians, who are seeking to promote the cause of Christ in a manner and with a devotion which we of another temperament and country can scarcely comprehend. Sunday is observed as a Christian holy-day in all places. The word of God is preached in every parish. Wherever you go you will find people going to Church, and some walk a great distance, and do not stay at home on account of disagreeable weather. The stores and public places are closed, and the Sunday laws are kept strictly during the time of divine services."[82] Speaking of the sterling honesty of the people and of their trust in each other, so that when they leave their houses, they hang up the key on the outside, Congressman S. S. Cox, says: "We left our umbrella in the cars (reaching Copenhagen); and as an illustration of the regard to the *meum et tuum* which obtains among these people, we afterwards found it at our hotel in Norway, forwarded as if it were actual property, and at a cost too small to record." The first

Protestant foreign mission, and the only one of the Protestant Church in the sixteenth century, was established by Swedish Lutherans. Since then their missions have reached all lands. No wonder that these pious Scandinavian Lutherans, out of their comparative poverty, giving so generously to carry the gospel to the heathen, resent as an abuse of Christian courtesy and charity, the

---

[82] Hand Book of Lutheranism. p. 125.

action of some American sects in treating them as heathen, and appropriating more money for their conversion than they do for the dark continent of Africa.

Of Germany, in the Seventeenth Century, when the Lutheran type of piety was very marked and prevalent, Kahnis writes: "In the houses Bible and hymn book were the first and the last, the most faithful advisers in all the events of life. In the higher, as well as in the elementary schools, the confession of the fathers was considered as the chief knowledge; to be regular in attending the house of the Lord, and in coming to the table of the Lord, formed part of the family honor. All the ordinances of rank, of law, of the State, were connected with religion." [83] To-day, "Societies for the better observance of the Lord's day; for the promotion of temperance, the improvement of prison discipline and the care of dismissed convicts; the establishment of institutions for the laboring classes, colliers, sailors, orphans and the poor; and of asylums, hospitals, and deaconess homes; and all the efforts and means for the moral and religious reformatory movements, which are comprehended under the name of Inner Mission, are multiplying in every quarter."[84]

American Christians with Puritanic and anti-Lutheran prejudices who visit Europe often bring back unfavorable reports as to the state of religion in Lutheran lands and capitals. A few facts are quite sufficient to refute these prejudiced misrepresentations. Thus, it is charged that Berlin is an utterly irreligious city and that Christianity and the Church are there destitute of life and activity. Yet there are at present 26 Churches in process of erection in Berlin, and some of these so large that most of our edifices in comparison are but chapels. Where can such Church Extension activity be surpassed? And in each of these great Churches there are held numerous successive services on the Lord's day, and frequently during the week. The lack of Church accomodations is often spoken of as a matter of

---

[83] History of German Protestantism, p. 251.

[84] Hand Book of Lutheranism, p. 14.

reproach to these Lutheran lands. Yet a late number of the Independent' shows that the German Empire has a Protestant (Lutheran) population of 30,964,274, and 24,996 Protestant houses of worship, i. e., one Church for every 1,240 people, old and young. This is amply sufficient. As a matter of fact, taking the adults alone, the ratio is, in Prussia, one Church to 435, in Denmark, one to 400, and in Wurtemberg, one to 337. No better and more sufficient Church accommodations than these can be found elsewhere. This Churchly piety extends from the hut to the throne. Not only are the Lutheran Emperor and Empress regular worshipers, but they show the liveliest interest in Christian and Churchly enterprises, and sustain them by princely gifts of private generosity. "The Lutheran Church in Prussia embraces 6,900 pastoral charges, 200 of which were organized within the last four years. The annual number of confirmations is 318,000. There are 2,200 young men studying for the ministry in this Church. The gifts made in 1891 for the charitable objects of the Church amounted to $1,050,000. "Out of a Protestant population of 18,000,000, statistics show that 5,980,140 had communed within the last year—a better showing than this country can make. Of the Protestant population of the United States only one-fifth are communicants, and in Prussia we have one-third of the population not merely entitled to communion, but actually participating in the Lord's Supper within a year."[85] For the whole empire the average of those confirmed who communed was 48J per cent., 9 per cent being the lowest, and 81 per cent, being the highest. The notable feature, however, was that the lowest percentage was at Hamburg, where liberalism has made the greatest inroads and where confessional Lutheranism is weakest. And the very highest averages were maintained in the strictly Lutheran parts of the empire, and among the separatist Lutheran congregations, as the one at Zwickau.

The same is true of Lutherans in the United States, that they constitute the most reliably industrious and religious elements of the population, and that their quiet and unobtrusive, but thorough piety,

---

[85] Rev. G. F. Behringer in Lutheran Observer.

is every day being more felt and acknowledged. "The real judgment of the vigor of our spiritual life is based upon a comparison with the spiritual life of present religious bodies. As compared with them, the result is on the whole favor

able. Our Church is respected and esteemed by the best ministers and best members of other Churches. It has not only now place and recognition, but maintains them with increasing power."[86]

The Lutheran Church is the parent of modern evangelical missions. A Lutheran King of Denmark sent the first Protestant Missionaries to India, where the name of the Lutheran Schwarz yet lives among the Christian natives in undying fragrance. And "the Lutheran Church was carrying forward on a vast scale a successful mission in India one hundred years before any of the English Churches had a single missionary station in heathen lands."[87] The Herrmansburg Missionary Society in Germany, founded by the Lutheran, Harms, has been so wonderfully blessed, and the means of sending out so many missionaries to heathen lands, as to win the envious title: "The Wonder of the Mission World." And the first religious book translated for the evangelization of our American Indians was Luther's Catechism, by Campanius, a Swedish Lutheran pastor. "The Lutheran Church has 40 chartered missionary societies at work among the heathen. These societies have 185 stations in Asia, 505 in Africa, and 12 in Australia. On these 700 stations, occupied as centres of mission labor, there are 1,000 missionaries, 100 native preachers, and 4,000 other native helpers. On the 700 mission stations, there are 210,000 members, 1,000 schools, and 60,000 pupils. The annual income of the societies is $1,200,000. Its fields of Labor are: Japan, Southern China, Sumatra, Borneo, Farther India, Central and Southern India, Persia, Palestine, in Asia; Bogss-land, Galla-land, German East Africa, Madagascar, Natal, Transvaal and Orange Free State, Cape Colony, Namaqualand, the Congo, the

[86] Rev. C. S. Albert, D.D., in Lutheran Observer.

[87] Lutherans in America—Wolf, p. 494.

Cameroons and Togeland, Slave Coast, Gold Coast, Liberia, Senegambia, in Africa; Queensland, New Zealand and New Guinea, in Australia. Greenland and Lapland are not counted in, because they are almost Christianized—thro' her efforts."[88]

The first and greatest Orphan Asylum, was founded in a Lutheran Country, Halle, Germany, and by a Lutheran, Francke. At his death it provided for 2,000 orphans, and it has been the blessed seed of similar institutions now scattered all over the world.

The institution of Protestant Deaconesses, resembling the Catholic sisterhoods of charity, was founded by a Lutheran pastor, Fliedner, at Kaiserwerth, Germany. From this beginning, in 1836. the order has spread through Germany, Switzerland, France, Scandinavia, Russia, Austria, England, and the United States, until there are now 65 Deaconess Houses, with 8,678 sisters and 2,774 labor stations. "Germany," says the Independent, "leads all Christian countries in this work." The most splendid of these in the United States is the Mary J. Drexel Home and Mother House of Deaconesses at Philadelphia, founded by the gift of $500,000, and supported by its Lutheran founder, John D. Lankenau, Esq., while he lives. In all, there are sixty-six Orphans' Homes, Deaconess Houses, etc. in the United States.

The Lutheran piety, then, is the brightest gem in her coronet of Christian graces. It is joyous, as well as stable; practical, while Churchly and "conservative; and knows how, from the still closet of a holy mysticism, to go forth in the world and serve God with works of power. The purest orthodoxy should not be dead, but the tree that bears the best and most plentiful deeds of practical piety. Lutherans best serve their Church, and honor its faith, when "having the form of godliness they do not deny the power thereof," but when it can be said of them as of Luther that "the confessor of the righteousness of faith had what he confessed and was what he taught."

[88] Mission Tract, Dr. Wackernagel, Muhlenberg College.

CHAPTER XV.
CHRISTIAN NURTURE, OR CHILDREN IN THE LUTHERAN CHURCH

THE Lutheran Doctrine of Baptism involves the idea of Christian Nurture. It is that Baptism is to be applied to infants, and that Baptism is the beginning of the spiritual life. This holy beginning, or quickening, is thenceforward to be fostered and developed by the use of the means of grace. As intelligence dawns, the baptismal covenant is to be unfolded to the child, viz. that by it he is admitted into the kingdom of God and called to salvation and eternal life. Then by the Word, and later on by the Sacrament, the grace of his Baptism is to be nourished and strengthened on to full and ever-growing Christian stature. That is, the child's spiritual life is to repeat that of the holy and model child Jesus, viz. "And the Child grew, and waxed strong in spirit, filled with wisdom; and the grace of God was upon Him" (Luke 2:40).

The Scriptures consistently thus represent the spiritual life as a growth, a development, an orderly progress, after the semblance of the natural life. "So is the kingdom of God, as if a man should cast seed in the ground—and the seed should spring and grow up—first the blade, then the ear, after that the full corn in the ear" (Mark 4:26-28). Children, thus, being in the kingdom of God by baptism, and having the new spiritual life therein begun in them, are already in a state of grace. And all that they have to do is to "keep" and nurture that "good thing which was committed unto them by the Holy Ghost, which dwells in them" (2. Tim. 1:14). The theory of the Churches which deny baptismal grace and the beginning of the spiritual life therein, is that children are in a condition of spiritual death, out of which they must be aroused by some great and sudden spiritual excitement, conflict, and experience.

The decisive objection to this view is that it leaves children and youth during all their early years in the attitude of unregenerated souls, who, should they die, would die unconverted and be lost. And then it contradicts the scriptural order of the life of grace which is that of a gradual process of growth, instead of that of a sudden and violent change. The Lutheran idea, then, of Christian Nurture rests upon the idea that children in baptism are "planted in Jesus Christ our Lord and Savior," and that all through their early years this formative power of grace is developing them into spiritual manhood. They do not look forward to conversion, but God has already accepted them, and they enjoy the divine favor.

But here then comes the responsibility of parents and sponsors. If the new life is to be gradually developed during youth, and not to be suddenly acquired at a later period, then all the means of grace must be most carefully applied during this critical season. Hence the duty of Christian Nurture. For this, accordingly, the Lutheran Church makes careful provision. In the formula of baptism this obligation is thus urged: "I now admonish you, who have done so charitable a work to this child in its Baptism, that ye diligently and faithfully teach it, or have it taught, that it may learn to know the will of God, to obtain grace, and find help to lead a Christian life, till God shall perfect that which He hath now begun in it, and bring it to life everlasting." In order to fulfill this obligation there results the duty of religious instruction at home, in school, and in Church.

That this might be efficiently done Luther prepared the Catechism, wherein children should be taught in a plain and Scriptural manner the plan of salvation as exemplified in the Ten Commandments or Law, in the Creed or Gospel, in the Lord's Prayer, and in the Holy Sacraments as the Means of Grace. Of the great importance of this religious agency, Luther wrote: "The Catechism is the first and most important instruction for children. Catechization ought to be diligently practiced by every parent at home, and by every pastor in the Church. No one can become master of the whole catechism, and hence all the members of the Church should continue to study it. Let no one be ashamed of it, but adhere to it steadfastly, for it must remain and attain the ascendency in the Church, though earth and hell rage against it." The catechization of the young, then, their careful and systematic instruction in the elementary truths of Christianity and the order of salvation, is diligently practiced everywhere by the Lutheran Church. She believes that childhood and youth are the golden season to "Remember thy Creator," and the opportune age to find Him who has promised: "Those that seek Me early shall find me" (Prov. 8:17). And then, when the young intelligently comprehend their baptismal covenant, and are ready to ratify it for themselves, and are spiritually strong enough to run for themselves the Christian race, they come out and make their good confession at the altar by the holy rite of Confirmation. "The General Synod lays the utmost stress upon the duty of bringing up the young in 'the nurture and admonition of the Lord,' especially those to whom God, through holy baptism, has given the 'adoption of children,' that they may become, and truly be, in heart and life, all that is meant in their divinely-given Church-membership. As 'the force, value, and blessing of the baptismal covenant and grace are to extend through their whole subsequent lives,' the method of their proper care and spiritual development is regarded as distinctively educational, under the regenerating and sanctifying power of the Holy Ghost through the truth as it is in Jesus Christ. Catechization, therefore, is not looked upon as a mere routine formality, or a process of simply intellectual indoctrination, that shall, of course, terminate in confirmation, irrespective of genuine faith, spiritual interest, or a purpose of true Christian obedience on the part of the catechumens.[89]

The Lutheran Church has thus ever had a warm place in her fold for the tender lambs, and her whole history exemplifies those sweet words of Jesus: "Suffer the little children to come unto Me, and forbid them not; for of such is the kingdom of God" (Mark 10:14). "The Lutheran Church devotes her best strength to the

---

[89] "Distinctive Doctrines and Usages of Lutheran Bodies." Prof. M. Valentine, D.U., LL.D., pp. 51 and 52.

religious instruction and training of the young. She has in this land nearly 5,000 pastors annually catechizing them. She has nearly 500,000 scholars in Sunday Schools."[90] But her experience has been that valuable as is the Sunday School as a spiritual agency, yet the instruction given there but one hour in the week, and the catechetical teaching of the pastor, with the very little that too often alas! is imparted at home, is not sufficient to counteract the abounding worldly temptations and influences at work to weaken religious impressions. This is shown by the fact that so many of those confirmed after a short time relapse, and fall away from their good confession. Hence, in foreign lands, Lutheran children receive regular religious instruction as a part of their daily school curriculum for years both before and after confirmation.

And in America, where such religious instruction is not given in the Public Schools, to meet this want, there has arisen the Parochial School. This is a school in connection with a congregation, supported and managed by it. Of these Lutheran Parochial Schools there are about 3,000 in the United States, with about 300,000 scholars. In addition to secular instruction, the scholars are taught daily the Catechism, Bible History, the Life of Christ, Church History, the Reformation, the Augsburg Confession, etc. "In most of the non-religious subjects of instruction, the English [these are chiefly German schools,] tongue is used in the class-room." Writes one of their advocates: "We cannot be satisfied with having our children instructed an hour a week in matters that pertain to the eternal salvation of their immortal souls. We are convinced, and this conviction of ours is based upon experience, that if our children are to receive a thorough knowledge and lasting impression of the Bible, its divine truths and commandments, they are in need of daily religious instruction. The law of God will have to be called to their minds, explained to them, and brought home to their hearts day after day. Even the secular sciences taught in our schools are pervaded by a Christian spirit. That is what we, under present circumstances,

---

[90] The Lutheran Church—Schmauk, p. 9.

deem the best, if not the only correct method of bringing up our children in the nurture and admonition of the Lord; and that is the reason why we Lutherans make it a practice to establish, build, and maintain parochial schools."[91] When we see this motive and hear these plausible arguments, and remember the pious sacrifice prompting the support of these parochial schools, while the national public schools must be supported in addition, we cannot but admire the spirit shown.

The truth is the lack of religion in America as a part of the daily tutelage of the young is rapidly becoming one of the greatest problems of the hour. To it, more than to all other causes must be traced the growing irreligion of our youth, and the indifference of the masses to the Church. These evils are largely owing to the want of a specific system of Christian Nurture, such as prevails in the Lutheran Church. And what our Church in this country needs is to adhere to these judicious principles, and not alone to hold them in theory, but to reduce them to practice. The grave responsibility resting upon Lutheran pastors and parents, is to see to it that the children of the Church are not spiritually neglected, but that they grow up under such constant religious influences as shall hold them for Christ, and develop in them a strong and abiding Christian man and womanhood.

[91] Hand Book of Lutheranism, p. 420.

CHAPTER XVI.
OUR LUTHERAN YOUNG PEOPLE.

THE young people of the Lutheran Church considered as a distinctive class, have only come into prominence within the past few years, since our Church in common with all other denominations has realized the fact that the enlistment of her young people is necessary for the future welfare of the Church.[92]

Nothing has expressed this idea more forcibly than a paragraph appearing in one of the pamphlets issued by the Lutheran Young People's Association, of New York, which reads as follows: "All careful observers must admit that the efforts put forth by the Churches of all denominations to enlist the young people of their respective communities in the cause of Christ, are of the most vital importance to the successful evangelization of the world, because the young men and young women of every nation have in their keeping the destiny of that nation, and the result will be either for or against the Kingdom of Christ, just in the proportion in which the Churches have recognized and utilized these mighty forces for the work of that kingdom, or else have been recreant in their trust, and have allowed the spiritual life to become dormant. 'Whatsoever a man sows, that shall he reap,' is no truer of individuals than of Churches. That these facts are accepted as of supreme importance is attested by the establishment of National Associations for young people by many denominations. The Methodists have their Epworth League, the Episcopalians the Brotherhood of St. Andrew, the Baptists their

---

[92] This chapter is contributed, at the author's request, by E. F. Eilert, President of The Luther League of New York, and Editor of "Luther League Review."

Baptist Union, and the Roman Catholics a very strong National organization, while the Society of Christian Endeavor, and Young Men's Christian Associations, although undenominational in character, are wielding an influence that has been felt the world over. The Lutheran Church, however, has exceptional opportunities for reaching and keeping her young people loyal to the Kingdom of the Savior. Her Sunday School system, supplemented by a six months' course of catechetical instruction, and culminating in confirmation, gives her, when faithfully carried out, an immense advantage over other denominations. Unfortunately, she has never made the fullest use of her opportunities, owing partly to mistaken zeal and conflicting languages, but mostly to neglect and indifference."

Appreciating these opportunities, while deploring the losses heretofore sustained, the young Lutherans of New York City about five years ago laid the first stone in the construction of a distinctive Lutheran Young People's Union, which should unite in a common bond of fellowship and mutual esteem, the young people of all the various divisions of our Church.

The success of the Central Association thus formed was soon manifest, and after a few years trial in their own locality, the work was extended and plans made for the establishment of similar Central Associations throughout the country.

In the plea issued for this work the following appeared:
"One of the greatest evils the Lutheran Church has to contend with is the proselyting of its young people by other denominations. It has been said that the best material for Church workers is to be found among the young Lutherans, and consequently they are much sought after. As the Lutheran Church has offered little inducement and encouragement for the usefulness of the younger element, it is not surprising that so many are taken away from her year after year, and become active in Churches of other denominations and among societies connected therewith. The plan of forming Central Associations of the Young People's Societies, existing in certain localities, and urging these Central bodies to see to it that a Young People's Society is to be found in every Lutheran Congregation in that locality, or district, is one of the remedies that has been offered to overcome this great evil."

The plan has met with favor and already a number of Central Associations have been established in many States, more particularly in New York State, where the work has been given special attention, resulting in the establishment of a New York State Association, called the Luther League of New York. While the movement has been centered largely in the East, it is gaining ground all over the country, and the organization of other State Associations and the formation of a National Union is only a question of a short time. By these means it is intended to have our Lutheran young people organized as thoroughly as any of the other denominations and unitedly work for the upbuilding of the Church and the advancement of Christ's Kingdom.

Certainly these efforts should meet with the hearty approval of all our pastors and congregations, and the time be looked forward to with lively anticipation when our young people will be organized into one grand National body.

In the Lutheran Churches, unlike those of other denominations in this respect, we find various forms of associations, each congregation having such organization as it deems most suitable for the particular field in which it is located. The Christian Endeavor Society may be found in a number of congregations, more particularly among Churches of the General Synod. The Luther Alliance is a form of organization first inaugurated in one of the Synods of Pennsylvania. It uses a liturgical form of worship and adopts a particular constitution. The Alliance form has met with favor in many quarters.

The form of association which is most common among Lutheran Churches is the Young People's Society. It is conducted as other Church organizations, and is usually led by the pastor of the congregation.

These organizations are adapted to the individual requirements of the congregation with which they are connected, their sphere, in some instances, being larger than in others, but as a usual thing having the care of the young people as their particular mission. Among the German Lutheran Churches, the Young Men's Association predominates, but usually Young Ladies' Societies are also connected with these congregations. Their work is, as a rule, similar to that of Young People's Societies.

In the western part of New York State more especially than elsewhere, the beneficiary plan is used by a number of Young Men's Associations. These benevolent associations particularly aim to keep within the folds of the Church the young men who would otherwise join beneficiary orders or institutions.

An examination of these beneficiary organizations reveals the fact that two-thirds are German in language and membership, and consequently draw their members largely from our German Churches. Among the Central Associations of Lutheran Young People already organized all the forms of organization alluded to will be found. It is not intended to recommend any of the particular types of associations, as each pastor and congregation is better able to judge the requirements of their particular Church and adopt the best form that is to be had.

All associations of young Lutherans, no matter by what name the association is known, as long as they are connected with an Evangelical Lutheran Church, are entitled to membership in a Central Association. The Young People's movement which is so rapidly developing at present in the Lutheran Church is sui generis. Unlike many other denominations our young people make no claim to any "new" or improved method of spreading the Gospel, or of building up the Church, but rely exclusively upon the preached Word and the faithful use of the Sacraments for the propagation of the faith. Occupying a unique position, midway between pietistic separatism on the one hand, and the torpid inertia resultant from formalism on the other, this movement will be watched with interest by the whole Church, and the reflex influence of "youthful enthusiasm" cannot fail to stimulate the zeal of the older people.

CHAPTER XVII.
THE LUTHERAN CHURCH AND CULTURE.

GERMANY represents the highest standpoint of intellectual culture attained in the history of the human race. "The Germans," says Emerson, "are the modern Greeks, the intellectual masters of the world." "As Israel was elected to prepare the true religion for the world, Greece to develop the principles of science and art, Rome to actualize the idea of law and civil government —so in our times the chief significance of Germany lies in science and literature."[93] As Germany originated the Reformation, and thereby revolutionized the modern history of man, so has she been the center of the greatest thought movements of the age. Her thinkers are in the forefront in every problem of mind, and her scholars take the lead in every department of investigation and knowledge. In theology, in philosophy, and in science, the Germans are the leaders. "The German mind has been so productive in almost all branches of literary effort, that the annual issues of the German Press have numbered many thousands.

In philosophy the first name in the order of merit is that of Immanuel Kant. A powerful impulse was given to the study of history by Niebuhr. German researches have been carried into every region of the past. A host of German scholars have engaged in the investigation of the origin and interpretation of the Bible. In Biblical criticism, Ewald, Tischendorf, Meyer, Weiss, are theological scholars familiar to Biblical students in all countries. German travelers have explored many countries of the globe. Schliemann has uncovered the ruins of Troy. In mathematics and the natural sciences, in philology

---

[93] Germany and its Universities—Schaff, p, 8.

and criticism, in philosophy, in law and the political sciences, and in the different branches of theology, the world acknowledges its debt to the patient, methodical investigations, and the exhaustive discussions of German students during the present century."[94]

Says Joseph Cook: "Germany is the most learned nation on the globe. The leading books in every scholar's library are written by Germans." In 1892 America published 4,559 books, France 4,000, England 5,735, while Germany published 21,279, more than all the others together, and of a more scholarly order. Germany is the modern Athens—the literary center toward which the students of all countries flock to complete a cultured education. The universities of Germany are the best equipped, attended by the largest number of students, and the most renowned in the world. In the year 1892, 30,000 students attended the German universities, as against but 5,500 students at Oxford and Cambridge, England. The Independent says: "The German universities are the most cosmopolitan institutions of learning in the world. They draw students literally from every cultured land and climate. Of the 29,518 students matriculated at these high schools during the present term no fewer than 1,948 are foreigners." "The universities are the pride and glory of Germany. They are the centers of the highest intellectual and literary life of the nation, and the laboratories of new systems of thought and theories of action. They reflect a picture of the whole world of nature and of mind under its ideal form." [95] Germany has the lowest ratio of illiterates in the world. In the Lutheran kingdom of Wurttemberg in every 10,000 persons, there are only 2 who cannot read and write, while in the United States there are 1,700 in every 10,000, or a ratio 850 times as great.[96]

[94] Universal History, Prof. Fisher, Yale College, p. 629.

[95] Germany and its Universities—Schaff, p. 27.

[96] United States Census on Illiteracy for 1880.

And as Germany is the origin and chief center of the Lutheran Church, it is inevitable that this same literary pre-eminence should characterize this communion. As a rule, the great universities are either exclusively Lutheran, or Lutheran professors have a controlling influence. The greatest theologians and biblical scholars have been those of the Lutheran Church. "German theological science comes forth from the Lutheran Church. The theology of the Lutheran Church supported by German diligence, thoroughness, and profundity, stage by stage, amid manifold struggles and revolutions, arose to an amazing elevation, astounding and incomprehensible to the Swiss, the French, and the English."[97]

"The Lutheran Church," says the Reformed Lange, "is the Church of theologians." "Her universities," writes Dr. Seiss, "have been the glory of Germany for the last three hundred years; and her critics and religious teachers have been the leading instructors of Christendom from the days of Luther until now. Take from the religious literature of the nations all that has been, directly or indirectly, derived from Lutheran divines, and the ecclesiastical heavens would bebereft of most of its stars. Strike out the long list of Lutheran names and writings, in whatever department, which each of these past three centuries has furnished, and a void would be made for which all the ages could produce no adequate compensation."[98] "The first," says Dr. Wolf, "to liberate the human mind from mediaeval darkness and error, the Lutheran Church has always fostered thorough intellectual culture. Her scholars have within the present century restored the glories of the best age of Christian learning. Her wonderful literature, her great universities, her systems of popular education are felt by the world."[99]

---

[97] Goebel, pp. 263, 267, quoted in Krauth's Conservative Reformation.

[98] Ecclesia Lutherana, p. 127.

[99] Lutherans in America, p. 476.

Prof. Painter, of Roanake College, in his work "Luther on Education," shows that Luther, by his efforts to adapt instruction to children, his reorganization of schools, introducing graded instruction, improved courses of study, etc., laid the foundation of the modern educational system, which begins with the common school and ends with the university. "'The German common schools, dating from Luther, may claim to be the oldest in Europe or America.'"[100] Thus the Lutheran Church, through her many-sided and farseeing founder, and through her literary outfit in Germany has really given the world the system of public schools, as well as the great university. "Perhaps in our practical Church work we do not sufficiently appreciate the fact that the Evangelical Lutheran Church, in her origin, history and character, is Germanic, just as the Episcopal and Methodist Churches are English, and the Presbyterian is Scotch. As the doctrinal system of a Church penetrates a nation, so the national and ethnological characteristics of a nation impress themselves upon the Church. So, through centuries, Lutheranism, more than anything else, has made the Germans and Scandinavians what they are, and it is natural that the human elements of Lutheranism should be Germanic. It is not an accident that the Germanic populations should feel most at home in the Lutheran Church, and that the Lutheran Church has her greatest success among these people."[101]

The same literary activity characterizes the Lutheran Church in America. In the face of the greatest disadvantages, its scholarly ideal has moved it to the establishment of manifold colleges, theological seminaries, and religious periodicals, and to the formation of a distinctive Lutheran literature ever becoming more worthy of its historic character.

---

[100] Dr. J. M. Gregory, Address to National Educational Association of the U. S., endorsed and circulated as an official paper by our Government.

[101] Rev. J. N. Lenker, in the Lutheran World.

This high degree of literary culture in the Lutheran Church naturally influences her methods. Large intelligence leads to moderation and enlightened judgment. The emotional and sensational religious methods, begotten of ignorance and illiteracy, are foreign to her. The culture of her ministry and of her people lifts them quite above these weak and ephemeral means. Accordingly, in her preaching, in her liturgical worship, in her methods of evangelization, everything "is done decently and in order." There may be Churches that have more money, but not that have better judgment and taste than the Lutheran. There may be Churches that draw more largely the untutored and novelty loving throng who wander like ecclesiastical tramps from one sensational glare to another, but no one, we believe, has so solid, so regular, so quiet, orderly, and sensible a membership. The Lutheran Church, accordingly, flourishes best in the most highly cultivated communities, and naturally attracts the thoughtful and cultured classes.

Lutherans sometimes seem ignorant of this high character and standing of their own Church, and even seem to think slightingly of it as compared with others. But the truly enlightened and cultured of other Churches put a very different estimate on the Lutheran Church. They look up to it with the greatest respect, and to them one can bring no higher claim for regard than to say: "I am a Lutheran."

To belong to a Church, the theological preceptress of the world, the nursery of the foremost intellectual culture of the age, and that has among its members more crowned heads, more erudite scholars, and more cultivated peoples than any other, certainly has nothing in it to lower a Lutheran's proper self-esteem.

CHAPTER XVIII.
THE LUTHERAN CHURCH AND SACRED ART.

NO factor, in every age, has had a more potent, influence upon the emotions of men than Art—the representation by material objects and emblems of the true and beautiful. In a large sense, Nature herself is supreme Art, for all the lovely and varied forms of Nature are types, symbols, and signs, of the invisible world of thought. Inevitable is it, therefore, that Art should have a place in connection with Religion, and be taken into its employ as its handmaiden and servant. The truest, highest Art is that which leads the imagination toward the invisible by means of the visible—that which makes Nature a stepping stone to the Creator. Hence, the prominent place which Art has occupied in all the natural religions, those "growing wild." "It is an immutable truth that Art and Religion are inseparably united. Through music, poetry, painting, sculpture and architecture, the spiritual can appeal directly to the human soul with a force that is irresistible. The Cathedrals and Churches of Europe, solemn and majestic, full of dim light and strange stillness, with their splendid ritual, have done much toward the spread and preservation of Christianity. Art is the ready servant and ally of the Church, and never have her proffered services, in the shape of ritual and adornment, been accepted without vast benefits, as, on the other hand, never have they been rejected without corresponding loss."[102]

   With the appearance of Revelation we find this agency at once utilized. The Old Testament Religion was set in the framework

---

[102] The Architectural Record, Vol. II, No. 3, p. 352.

of Art. Symbols were everywhere employed as the teachers of sacred truth. The glittering Shekinah, or emblem of the divine glory; the altar, typifying the one great sacrifice for sin; the golden candlestick, a symbol of the holy light of revelation; all were of a "typical character, and eminently subservient to the religious instruction and benefit of mankind, by shadowing forth in their leading features the grand truths of the Christian Church."[103] Our blessed Lord illustrated the same general principles in His instructions. His system of teaching was largely parabolic. His most exquisite lessons were uttered in parables. The similitudes between nature and truth He artfully applied to moral uses. The Lily, the Vine, the Flowers of the field, the Wheat and the Tare, afforded Him apt object lessons. The book of Revelation most notably exemplifies this principle. It is chiefly constructed of religious symbology. From first to last, it is a grand and majestic gallery of sacred art. The sublimest dispensations of God in the destiny of the Church, and in the fate of the world, are here painted in types and symbols on the canvass of inspiration.

How natural, then, that artistic representation of the true and divine should be enlisted in the service of Christianity. And history shows this to be the case. The earliest illustrations we have, of course, are in the Catacombs. Says the Church historian, Kurtz: "The great abundance of paintings on the walls of the catacombs, of which many belong to the second century, some indeed, perhaps, to the last decades of the first century, served to show how general and lively was the artistic sense among the earliest Christians." [104] These catacombs where the persecuted Christians fled, were really Churches, containing their sanctuaries of worship, and their altars on which were celebrated the Holy Sacrament. The artistic designs were numerous symbolical devices of the Christian faith. The principal one, however—in the desire to reproduce which, beyond doubt, all Christian Art originated —was the figure of Jesus Christ. He is

---

[103] Jamieson-Fausset-Brown Commentary, p. 65.

[104] Church History, Vol. I, p. 215.

represented in all conceivable Scripture forms, the one most in favor being that of the Good Shepherd. When, after the victory of Christianity through Constantine, Churches were built and ecclesiastical art more developed, "the center of the whole house of God was the altar, since the fifth century, commonly of stone, often overlaid with gold and silver."[105] In the great Cathedrals of the Middle Ages the instinct for Christian Art embodied itself in those imposing edifices which will forever remain the noblest monuments of the genius of man, exalted by the sentiment of pious devotion. The loftiest of these is the magnificent Lutheran Cathedral at Ulm, begun in 1377 and completed in 1889, holding 30,000 people, adorned with the richest paintings and sculptures, and with a spire of 540 feet, 28 feet higher than the famous Cologne Cathedral.

In the Reformation two typical leaders were at the helm. One of these was Luther, the other Zwingli, and later, Calvin. Luther, as the larger personality, the more eminent Christian, and the more intensely human and genial, naturally favored Art. He had a poetic soul, and a mystical devotion, which interpreted the divine and infinite, in all the forms of nature and art. Accordingly, he writes: "It is not my opinion that the arts are to be destroyed by means of the Gospel, as some super-spiritualists [Zwingli, Carlstadt, etc.] give out, but I should like to see all the arts enlisted in the service of Him who has given and created them."[106] On the specific point as to the representation of Christ in the Church, which was in dispute between the Lutheran and the Reformed Churches, Luther makes this striking argument: "The Scripture has pictures. Hence I may for the sake of memory and a better understanding, paint them on the wall. In like manner, when I contemplate the sufferings of Christ, there projects itself in my heart the picture of a man hanging upon the cross. Now, if it is no sin that I have the picture in my heart, why should it be a sin if I have it in the eye, especially when the heart is of more

[105] Church History, Kurtz, Vol. 1, p. 384.

[106] Luthardt's Moral Truths of Christianity, p. 391.

importance than the eye?" This fine answer, says Dr. Dorner, "decides the relation of [Lutheran] Protestantism to Art. The poetic, genial, and ideal feeling of Luther will as little dispense with the divine gift of painting as music, but will rather see them employed in the interest of religion."[107] Never had a man a greater temptation to go to an extreme. Zwingli, Carlstadt, and the Reformed, cried out that these artistic devices were Romish, and the paintings were torn from the walls, and the crosses broken on the altars. But Luther, with true wisdom, refused to argue from the abuse of a good principle against its proper use. In indignant protest he denounced these fanatical extremists, in a series of sermons of burning eloquence and power. And he judiciously selected the golden mean.

While Zwingli thus wished to do away with organ playing, instrumental music, etc., and Calvin would not tolerate altars, crosses, and candles, in the Churches, a wise moderation prevailed in the Lutheran Church. The principles of the great founder of Protestantism passed over to the Church called after his name. "In Romish worship all appealed to the senses, and in that of the Calvinistic Churches all appealed to the understanding; but in the Lutheran worship both sides of human nature were fully recognized, and a proportionate place assigned to each. Altars ornamented with candles and crosses were allowed to remain, not as objects of worship, but rather to aid in exciting and deepening devotion."[108]

This employment of sacred art in the building of Churches, and in their interior and altar appointments and decorations, has accordingly become characteristic of Lutheran, as contrasted with Calvinistic and Reformed Churches all over the world.[109] The only

---

[107] History of Protesting Theology, Vol. 1, p. 146.

[108] Church History, Kurtz, Vol. II, p. 364.

[109] "The Lutheran Church designates different colors for the different seasons of the year, so that the Church's joy or sorrow may be taught by the eye as well as by the ear. These various colors, used in the several services of the Church, are all symbolical and add solemnity to the devout worship

exception is that of the Episcopal Church, where these artistic uses were borrowed from the Lutheran, and not borrowed by us from the Episcopal, as is sometimes supposed by the misinformed. Their Lutheran origin is fully admitted by the distinguished Episcopal scholar, Dean Stanley. Speaking of the changes which occurred in Queen Elizabeth's time, he writes: "The Lutheran element remained too strongly fixed to be altogether dislodged. Lutheranism was, in fact, the exact shade which colored the mind of Elizabeth, and of the divines who held to her. Her altar was the Lutheran altar."[110] "In her doctrine Elizabeth was a moderate Lutheran.

Dr. Schaff not only admits this distinction of sacred art as belonging to the Lutheran, as over against the other Protestant Churches, but really accords it the superiority, thus: "Lutheranism draws the fine arts into the service of religion. The Reformed communion is much poorer in this respect. It aimed at the greatest simplicity in religion, which in Presbyterianism and Puritanism is certainly carried to excess. Mrs. Beecher Stowe, though herself a Puritan, in describing the wondrous beauties of nature in Switzerland, worship, molding and tincturing religious thought in all communions, have to the present time, prevented the Lutheran Church from assuming her true place with respect to the use of sacred art. It is, as Dr. Wolf truly remarks in his review of Dr. Schaff's Church History in the Lutheran Quarterly, January 1893: "One of the most instructive features of this volume is its disclosure of the truth that

---

of Almighty God in His house. White is a symbol of purity, joy, life, and light, and is used on the Festivals of Christmas, Easter, and the Ascension of our Lord, and on Whit-Sunday, on Trinity Sunday, and on the dedication of a Church. Violet or Purple, the symbol of penitence and sorrow, is used during Advent and Lent Seasons, and at funerals. Green, the symbol of hope and peace, and Red, the symbol of divine love and royal dignity, are used from Trinity Sunday until Advent. Black, the symbol of death, is used on Good Friday."—The Church Year, Rev. W. H. Gotwald, D.D.

[110] Christian Institutions, p. 89.

almost all those things against which Lutherans have to battle incessantly within their own Church, are importations from the Churches of Zwingli and Calvin. The Puritans brought with them to this country the favorite ideas and practices of these Reformers so far as they antagonized the Lutheran Reformers, and when our feeble English Churches were struggling for existence, they somehow fell into the ways of Calvinism—probably because their pastors had received their training from Calvinist schools and Puritan authors. The denial of quickening grace in Baptism, of the Real Presence in the Eucharist, the opposition to pictures in the Churches, to altars, crosses, candles, clerical robes, etc., have come to us from either Zwingli, or Calvin, or both."

While the whole history of the Lutheran Church thus shows her distinctive attitude and practice, as appreciative of the positive uses and benefits of sacred art. and while the advocacy of these principles is especially needed at this time to counteract prevalent prejudices, yet the Lutheran Church would none the less protest against making them essential and binding upon the conscience. Sacred Art, however important, still rests upon the grounds of expediency, and as such, belongs to the sphere of liberty. Hence the Lutheran Observer is quite correct in this recent editorial: "However, the whole matter of Church decoration with Christian symbols and other works of art within appropriate limits, belongs to the adiaphora, or things indifferent and non-essential, and these are free to be used or not, according to the taste or preference of congregations, so far as not forbidden in the Scriptures."

The ground of these objections is laid upon Romish and Ritualistic abuses. But these objections would on the same ground sweep away the essentials of Christianity. The Scriptures, the Sacraments, the Apostle's Creed, the Festivals, the rite of Confession, the authority of the Church, are all similarly abused in the Romish Church. Dare we, therefore, reject them? Whatever then is right, and true, and useful in itself, we are not to discard, because of perversions and excesses, but we are to use so judiciously as to avoid and reprove those abuses.

So with Art, as related to Religion. It is natural, sustained by Scripture analogy, employed by Christ, and an invaluable aid to devotion. It is Christian, having characterized the entire history of the Christian Church. Moreover, it is specifically Lutheran, distinguishing the Lutheran from all the Reformed Churches in this regard. Now, the question for us, as Lutherans, here in America, is this, Will we, as we sometimes heretofore have done join our ecclesiastical opponents in decrying our own historic usages? If so, let us remember, that "A house divided against itself shall not stand" (Matt. 12:25). Our Churches here cannot be built up from anti-Lutheran elements. We may discard ever so much to please them; they will still stay in their own native and powerful Churches. But our Lutheran sons and daughters have been used to a well-defined ecclesiastical art from whatever part of our worldwide Church they have come. They bring these fond and sacred associations with them, and if we will reject Lutheran Churches and altars, and other Churches will adopt them, we can only expect that they will go where they feel at home. And then that irony of American history will repeat itself, that, when other Churches have drawn the intelligent and cultured by the use of our Lutheran customs, and have grown powerful thereby, we will timidly begin to dare to use them ourselves. And then the objection will be raised that we are borrowing the customs of others.

Why not be the first ourselves to use our own precious historic treasures, and then when others want them, compel them to be the borrowers? How far better thus to evince a manly self-respect and courage! And instead of apologizing for, or rejecting our Lutheran heritage, let us boldly espouse it, and proudly hold it up to the world as without a peer. Christendom will only respect the Church which first respects itself. The Lutheran Church with regard to Sacred Art, like so many other things, has nothing to be ashamed of. On the contrary, her history here shows her to be in harmony with primitive usage, with Scripture, and with the most cultured minds and gifted souls of the human race. Of no Lutheran feature can we have a more just pride, none is in closer touch with the trend of modern thought, nor is there one that will more recommend her as the Church worthy to be a leader of the Church Universal. Her motto is: "In Christianity, pictorial and sculptured representations, are language made visible, symbolized thought, divine lessons presented through the eye, which God has made an organ for the reception of truth as well as the ear.

Lutheran Churches are sanctuaries where on every side religion breathes, sacred visions hold the eye, whispers of the divine reach the soul, and the footseps of God grow audible. The Lutheran altar[111] is a veritable Holy of Holies, a staircase to the invisible, a place where the soul communes with the glorified Savior, and bathes in the light of infinite love. In the Lutheran Sanctuary, Art uses her every gift to make audible and visible the truths of Christianity, and to invest, with a rich and sacred halo, the sentiment of Religion.

As an instructive illustration of the manner in which the Lutheran Church, in its attitude respecting Sacred Art, is in sympathy with the best progressive tendencies of the age, we append to this chapter the following extract from a valuable paper on this theme, which recently appeared in that widely circulated religious publication, "The Homiletic Review:" "The conclusion of these phases of the whole subject is, that paintings, pictures, reproductions of the pathos and power of many of them, have been positive means of Christian education, thorough conversions, and the perseverance in saintliness of the persons thus converted. Savanarola, in the cloisters and cells of his convent, was deeply moved by the paintings of Angelico, whose art was worship and for the advancement of the Church. Zinzendorf, the founder of the first Protestant missionary Church, was converted by contemplating a picture of the crucifixion, which bore the inscription:

'I did this for thee;
What hast thou done for me?'

If there has been one offering on the altar of the Lord, which has has been devotional in aim and spirit equal to sacred music and poetry, it is sacred pictorial art. The Bible and the Christ have been

---

[111] The Lutheran Church is the only Protestant Church which strictly has an Altar, and uses that term in her formularies of worship. In the Episcopal Book of Common Prayer, the word "Altar" was stricken out by the Calvinistic revisers, and "Communion Table" substituted.

reproduced in this form according to the gifts bestowed by nature and by grace. Such portraiture has been given, and the objections to it are similar to the objections to written lives of Christ by Farrar and Edersheim, Geikie and Beecher, and to the sermons of the best preachers, and even to the records of the evangelists themselves. Protestantism in this particular has been wrong and Puritanism too. The reaction has been from one extreme to the other. There has been little attempt to gain and keep the golden mean."[112]

---

[112] New York, May, 1893.

CHAPTER XIX.
LUTHERAN UNITY.

WHEN our Lord prayed that all His disciples might be one, he evidently had two ideas chiefly in view, viz. spirituality and efficiency. For brotherly unity is necessary to piety. Where division, distraction, and strife prevail, there cannot be the sweet and peaceful spirit of Christ. And so efficiency in Christian work depends upon unity. As an army torn and sundered by internal dissensions can accomplish nothing against the foe,. so a Church rent by differences and controversy within its own borders, can do very little effective work for Christ. On this account, the various denominations have their separate confessions and usages, in order that those who are of one mind can work together in undisturbed harmony.

Now the Lutheran Church encounters exceptional difficulties in seeking to attain this unity. Its very strength is here a source of weakness. As it is so widely distributed throughout the various nationalities and languages of the globe, the problem becomes the more difficult to fuse all these types into one American Lutheran Church. Yet, on the other hand, there are several powerful conditions tending to facilitate this unity. One is the personality of Luther, which is so predominant and overshadowing among all Lutherans, as to be a perpetual force molding them alike, and so drawing them together. Another, is the doctrine of the Lutheran Church that unity does not depend upon secondary points, such as identity of Church government, or of rites and ceremonies. Differences on these adiaphora are no reason, therefore, to hinder true and hearty Lutheran unity. These must be regarded with mutual tolerance and charity. But even here Lutheran worship everywhere has been controlled by the type of Luther's Reformation Service, so that an essential historical unity of public worship characterizes Lutherans of all lands, drawing them together as one spiritual family.

Another impulse toward Lutheran unity comes from the singular pre-eminence of the Augsburg Confession. No other Church has any one summary of faith enjoying such a unique and universal authority over all its various branches, as does this venerable symbol. Not a solitary body of Lutherans rejects it. Nor does anyone propose its revision. Wherever there has been individual opposition to it, such opposition has been compelled to succumb to the overwhelming sentiment in its favor. "As various kingdoms, states, and cities, embraced the faith of God's word, as our Church had enfolded it, they accepted this Confession as their own, and were known as Evangelical Lutherans because they so accepted it. The Church was known as the Church of the Augsburg Confession. It is our shield and our sword, our ensign and our arming, the constitution of our state. It is the bond of our union throughout the world, and by it, and with it, our Church as a distinct organization, must stand or fall."[113]

The idea is sometimes entertained, that a serious difference exists among Lutherans on the ground that some subscribe the Augsburg Confession, and others to the Form of Concord. But this is a mistake. Those who in addition subscribe to the later symbols do not do so in any spirit of antagonism to the Augsburg Confession, but only because they deem the latter a consistent explanation and development of the Augsburg Confession, so that their subscription to them only more firmly seals their subscription to the Augustana. Thus says one whose general body demands, not of laymen, but of pastors and teachers, subscription to the Form of Concord: "Those who sincerely adopt the Confession of Augsburg and the Catechism, are in accord with us. Our controversy with those who reject a portion of the Confession, has its ground in the conviction that such rejection betrays a dissent from the Evangelical doctrine set forth in the Augsburg Confession, whose true import and meaning the later

---

[113] Conservative Reformation, Krauth, pp. 262 and 214.

symbols develop and defend."[114] He, then, who heartily receives the Augsburg Confession, in the sense in which our Church has always received it, is a Lutheran, and no one dare gainsay his Lutheranism. Just as un-Lutheran, are extra and supra-confessional tests and conditions as is an infra-confessional laxity.

As therefore, the Augsburg Confession is thus generally and heartily accepted by Lutherans, there is more true unity and agreement in faith and spirit among Lutherans than in any other Christian body in the world. Writes one of our divines of this theological unity: "As we have reason to know, the doctrine of the Real Presence is now taught in all Lutheran theological seminaries in this country, and is held, by the vast majority of the Lutheran pastors. And as Luther's Small Catechism, in its pure text, is used almost universally in Lutheran congregations as a manual of instruction, the doctrine is taught to the young people who are in preparation for the duties and benefits of Church membership."[115] Consequently, it is a matter of certainty, that a number of Lutherans assembled together from the widespread branches of Lutheranism throughout the world, could draw up a set of articles of common doctrinal agreement, and would find themselves in a harmony of spirit, such as could no other Church. A remarkable illustration of this truth is given in the volume that has lately appeared: "Distinctive Doctrines and Usages of the General Bodies of. the Evangelical Lutheran Church in the United States."[116] Six of the foremost theologians there speak for the bodies they represent, comprising 1,019,323 of our Lutheran communicants in the United States. And when we consider the amount of doctrinal divergence and looseness prevalent in the other denominations in our land, the positive hold upon the great Scriptural truths, and the close general doctrinal concurrence exhibited in this volume, constitute the

---

[114] Prof. M. Loy, D.D., of Joint Synod of Ohio.

[115] Rev. J. W. Richard, D.D.

[116] Lutheran Hoard of Publication, 42 N. Ninth St., Philadelphia.

religious phenomenon of the times. All these representative Lutheran theologians agree: a. In making the Word of God the supreme and only infallible rule of faith and practice, "while the symbols [confessions] are not considered like the Scriptures, as judges, but as a witness and declaration of the faith."[117] b. All accept the Augsburg Confession, without reservation, as, from beginning to end, "a correct exhibition of the fundamental doctrines of the divine word and of the faith of our Church,"[118] and "recognize the fact that the Evangelical Lutheran Church had her settled faith, and her distinctive character, when she witnessed her good confession at Augsburg, in 1530." "The question as to whether one be a Lutheran or not, the General Council affirms, must be decided from his relation to the doctrines of the unaltered Augsburg Confession, and from no other standard whatever."[119] c. All are one in the point that Christian unity is a matter primarily of agreement in the faith, and that rites and ceremonies, forms of worship, systems of Church government, etc., are secondary, and belong to the adiaphora (things indifferent). "Christians may differ, and in many cases, owing to different circumstances, must differ as to ceremonies, external organization, etc. But there is one thing concerning which all Christians of all times and of all countries should perfectly agree—they should be one in faith and doctrine."[120] d. And every one of these writers, while "never failing to distinguish between that which is necessary and that which is free," yet "love the old ways of our fathers, and the beautiful forms in which they worshiped the Lord." All " recognize the benefits of uniformity in the ceremonies and usages of the Churches, and heartily seek to promote it." All "desire, even in externals, to walk in

---

[117] Prof. S. Fritschel, D.D., p. 65.

[118] Prof. M. Valentine, D.D., LL.D., p. 41.

[119] Prof. H. E. Jacobs, D.D., LL.D., p. 57.

[120] Prof. F. Pieper, p. 137.

the old paths and manifest their historical connection with the old Church."[121]

Such a unanimity of sentiment—every writer, from what is generally considered the most moderate, the General Synod, to that which is commonly looked on as most extreme, the Synodical Conference, endorsing absolutely the one great Augsburg Confession in all its teachings, covering the whole main system of Scriptural doctrine—is a fact without parallel in any other denomination. No approach to such concurrence could be shown elsewhere. The bare thought of it would be considered utterly chimerical. "As to the substance of what is known as Lutheran all the writers agree. All accept the Augsburg Confession as the original and true confession of Lutheran doctrine, and consent that whoever heartily accepts the doctrinal statements of this Confession is a Lutheran, not in name, but in fact."[122] The evidences, then, in this remarkable series of papers, of essential unity on the part of the various Lutheran bodies of the United States, is one that should fill every Lutheran heart with encouragement, while it should attract the thoughtful attention and study of other bodies of Christians.

As a consequence of this fundamental unity, the Lutheran Church is the only branch of Protestantism that has never generated sects, not a single one having sprung from her, while the other wing of Protestantism has unfortunately had a multitudinous progeny of this character. In a recent editorial, "A Marvel in History," the Eastern Lutheran utters these indisputable words: "There has been no schism in the Lutheran Church from the beginning. There have been differences in language, and customs, and modes of worship, but there is only one Evangelical Lutheran Church in the world to-day. While the Lutheran half of Protestantism has come down unbroken through the centuries, the other half —the Reformed half—has been broken into fragments, and comprises all the other

---

[121] Prof. M. Loy, D.D., p. 10.

[122] The Lutheran World.

denominations of Christendom. It is reported that the census takers found 150 denominations, or sub-divisions of denominations, in this country, in 1890. The Lutheran Church is not responsible for the divisions of Protestantism. If the Augsburg Confession had been accepted by all in 1530, there might have been a unity of the Protestant Church to-day, as there is a unity of Catholicism. The fact that the Reformed part has broken into so many fragments, shows the weakness of its ecclesiastical platform. That the Lutherans have remained united for over three and a half centuries is a marvel, and it shows the strength of their ecclesiastical foundation."

These being the facts, there exists no sound excuse for our divisions in America. And as Dr. Jacobs truly says: "The problem of the hour for the Lutheran Church in America, is, how to unite these various elements in the historical faith of the Lutheran Church, as embodied in her historical confessions, and with the worship prescribed in her historical Liturgies and Church Orders."[123] The two greatest foes to this auspicious result are the extremists. The one, the party who would insist on extra-confessional and unhistorical tests. And the other, who are more eager to unite and fellowship with non-Lutherans than with those of their own household. Putting aside both these supra-and infra-Lutherans, why should not the Lutheran Church in this country be one?

In the Providence of God, despite all her mistakes and losses, she has now attained a commanding position here both theologically and numerically. She is known and recognized as one of the foremost ecclesiastical bodies of the land. But this lack of unity, and these contending General Bodies, with the synods and congregations maintaining an independent attitude, are our greatest element of weakness, and the chief obstacle in the path of our growth, success, and influence. Our sorest need is, as the patriarch Muhlenberg said: "Unity—a twisted cord of many threads will not break." God has laid upon us a weighty responsibility, as he has also given us an unrivalled opportunity in this Western World. And, bound together by such

---

[123] Preface to "The Lutheran Movement in England," p. 8.

strong and close ties of faith, usage and history, what we need above all things is to be one.

And to effect this we should not misrepresent our Lutheran brethern, of any branch or synodical connection of our Church, not seek to fan prejudices against them, and especially not take up the innuendoes and perversions of other denominations, and hurl them at those of our own faith and name. And by mutual charity, tolerance, sympathy, and good-will, we can come together, and work together, and march under the same banner, as one great, undivided Lutheran host, in this Western World. As indicative of the tendency at present prevailing, the Independent has lately had a colloquium of representative writers, on Lutheran Unity, in which Dr. Valentine for the General Synod, says: "Is the suggestion practicable? It ought to be. For these different bodies are all Lutheran bodies, the differences in their confessional basis being no greater than have always existed within the Lutheran Church. The points in disagreement, causing the divisions, do not belong to essentials. It were absurd for any one of these bodies to claim that its title to Lutheranism consists in the things in which it differs from all the other bodies. Its Lutheranism is made, not by the peculiarities in which it separates from all the rest, but by the truth and Church life which it maintains in common with them, the essential Lutheran system of doctrine." Dr. Jacobs, for the General Council, writes: "The Lutheran Church humbly claims to stand for the very widest basis possible for Christian union. Three centuries have passed, and the representatives of the various European Lutheran Churches are meeting in America. They have not come at once, but in successive waves of emigration, so that before one is organized and Americanized, it is overwhelmed by new accessions, among whom the same process is to be repeated. Who can be surprised that all are not united into one compact, homogeneous and well-organized general body? Has not much been gained, according to the showing of Dr. Carroll's statistics, that of 1,199,514 communicants 838,938 have been gathered into three general organizations?" Prof. Pieper, speaking for the Missouri Conference, after remarking various advances toward unification, says: "Still, there is a bad residue of divisions in the Lutheran Church, causing a great waste both of men and money. The gain to the

Lutheran Church would be enormous if a perfect consolidation in the Lutheran families could be effected. But how could this be done? The Lutheran Church has no peculiar ecclesiastical system nor any special rites to insist upon. All these things she classes with the 'adiaphora.' But the great stress is laid upon harmony in the Biblical doctrine. It was on this line of proceeding that practical results toward consolidation were obtained in the Lutheran Church. On this principle the Michigan Synod last year united with the Synodical Conference. Lately so-called "Free Conferences" were held between members of the Synodical Conference and other Lutheran bodies with the same object in view. Thus a campaign for consolidation is carried on."

Certainly, these are notable signs of the times. How much greater is the Lutheran unity prevailing now than a quarter of a century ago, and it is growing more and more every year. Instead of a dozen parties, each nursing its own narrow, little, one-sided, Lutheran phase, one supreme historical Lutheran ideal—the world-wide type —is gradually shaping all parties in accordance with it. And this is surely bringing all together. Lutheran unity is in the air! Nor can any petty, partisan narrowness withstand its advance. Let all join in the fervent hope expressed by Bishop von Scheele, during his visit among us, "that our great Church, in this country, might be united on the basis of the Augsburg Confession." Speed the grand consummation! Let every minister and every layman, instead of fomenting strife, and fanning the fire of prejudice, pray and strive for this auspicious end.

And with a united Lutheran Church in America, how nobly will our grand ecclesiastical mother take the leading position that belongs to her, how clearly will her testimony shine forth for the Word and Sacraments, and what effective service can she render for the advancement of the kingdom of God!

CHAPTER XX.
ENGLISH AND FOREIGN-SPEAKING LUTHERANS.

THE other Protestant Churches in the United States practically come from but one country, viz. Great Britain, and hence generally speak the English language. But Lutherans, coming from all the countries of Europe, predominantly speak foreign tongues. Prof. Boyesen estimates that nearly one-third of the population of New York City is German-speaking. In Chicago the proportion is about the same. The last decade brought a million and a half Germans to our shores. The great North West is filling up with Lutherans. Wisconsin alone has 150,000 German voters. There are more than one-third as many Norwegians here as in Norway. One half the population of Minnesota is Scandinavian. So marvelous has been our foreign growth in the great West that it is the surprising fact that there are 300 more Lutheran Churches west of Chicago than east of that city, and 80,000 more communicants. As a result, the Lutheran is the Church of many tongues in America.

The Government Census for 1890 thus tabulates Lutheran communicant members, according to language:
This table shows that the foreign-speaking Lutherans of America outnumber the purely English-speaking, in the proportion of 5 to 1. Or, in round numbers, there are only 200,000 English Lutherans, as against 1,000,000 speaking foreign tongues. With these foreign-speaking members, the Lutheran is one of the most powerful denominations in America; without them, one of the weakest and most insignificant. Now, the problem before the Lutheran Church is, how to effect the transition of these foreign-speaking members into the English-speaking Churches. Upon this, it is self-evident, depends

almost our very existence in the future. As our country fills up and emigration ceases, the foreign languages will inevitably die, and with them will also disappear the Churches using them. Lutheranism can only then survive in the English tongue. And every German, Swede, Norwegian, Dane, etc., who is a true Lutheran in heart, must desire before all else, the progress and welfare of the English Lutheran Church. The monument to perpetuate German and Scandinavian religious life and character in this country can never be language, it can alone be the faith and spirit of the Lutheran Church. As the Swedish Bishop von Scheele truly said in his address to the Swedish students of Bethany College, Lindsburg, Kansas, speaking of the question of language: "It lies in the very nature of the case that the rising generation should be taught in the English language, as any other course would, in America, be abnormal, since English is the language of America."

And the supreme difficulty that our English Lutheran Church encounters here, is the indifference, and often apparent antagonism, of our foreign-speaking members to our English Churches. For example, the Dutch Reformed, in point of numbers, are altogether insignificant in New York City, as compared with the German. Yet in that city, the Dutch Reformed have many more and more powerful English Churches than the Lutherans have. And simply because the Dutch were willing to surrender their language in order to save their Church. Their mother faith was dearer to them than their mother tongue. And until Germans, Swedes, etc., will rise to the same high standard, and illustrate their conviction that a Church is not to be restricted to one language, and not to be conditioned at all by language, but by faith, the progress of our Church in this country will continue to be arrested by this rock of stumbling. "For our true position and influence cannot be rightly achieved as a Church of an alien tongue or of alien tongues. However interesting and adapted to present necessities our Church's polyglot character may now be, the attainment of its right rank and influence in this country requires it to become as rapidly as possible an English-speaking Church."[124]

And yet the English Churches are here perhaps quite as much to blame as the foreign Lutheran element. They first set this mistaken example, that a change of language meant a change of Church. When they would establish a Church in the English language, too often they did not seek to make it a Lutheran Church, but in the process transformed it into a non-Lutheran one. Instead of merely changing the language, they changed the faith and historic usages. Thus in our early American history most of the characteristics of the world-wide Lutheran Church were dropped, and the peculiarities of the Puritan and Calvinistic Churches—repugnant to the broader, deeper, richer spirit of Lutheranism—were adopted. The beautiful and devotional liturgical service and worship of Lutheranism were discarded, and the worship framed after the non-Lutheran Churches. And shall we wonder, then, that when the foreign Lutheran cannot recognize his dear religious home, but discerns scarcely any difference between it and the non-Lutheran Churches, only that the latter are more numerous and powerful, more convenient of attendance, and offering greater social advantages, he should too often allow his children to go to them without a protest? When nothing of conscience, or of home-like feeling is to be gained, why make any sacrifice?

Until, then, the English Churches first lead the way by showing that a change of language does not involve an abandonment of Lutheranism. They cannot ask or expect foreign-speaking Lutherans to rally to their support. But if an English Church is Lutheran, if it is faithful to the Lutheran doctrine, and if it perpetuates that worship and those usages to which the Lutheran has been accustomed in his native land, then when the foreign Lutheran enters it, he will feel at home. And then, the bond of sacred traditions, childhood-memories, the love of fatherland, and early

---

[124] Prof. M. Valentine, D.D., I.L.D.. in "Distinctive Lutheran Doctrines and Usages," p. 57.

parental instructions, will draw him like an irresistible magnet to his own ecclesiastical altar.

Ignoring language then, alike by American and Foreigner, and making the Lutheran element supreme, alone lies the solution of this linguistic problem, which is the gravest practical one before us, dwarfing all others. But on the other hand, the question naturally arises: Shall we not have a distinctively American Lutheran Church here? We answer: Certainly, by all means. In every country our Church, even when built upon the great historic outlines of Lutheranism, will more or less in minor matters, be molded by, and reflect the genius and institutions of the land and race. It must have the quality of adaptation, which Lutheranism has shown itself to possess to a remarkable degree, or it could never have taken root in so many diverse lands. But to have such minor variations is one thing—to essentially transform the Lutheran character is another. The former only shows the flexibility and adaptedness of Lutheranism to world-wide conditions, and illustrates its .rightful claim to universal prevalence. The latter makes the Lutheran Church in one country a protest against the Lutheran Church of every other country, and so works for its injury and destruction. Some Lutherans in their intense Americanism forget that nationality has, as such, nothing to do with constituting a Church. Many Churches, thus, are Lutheran, but not American, such as the Lutheran Church of Sweden. And many Churches again are American, but not Lutheran, such as the Presbyterian Church. Faith and history, not nationality or language, constitute the distinctive features of a Church. Consequently, in order to be a Lutheran, it is not necessary to be a Germanu Swede, Dane, or Norwegian. Nor, in order to be an American is it necessary to drop Lutheran historical characteristics. True Lutheranism and true American ism make the ideal combination for our Church in America.

To blend all our foreign-speaking elements in one great English-speaking American Lutheran Church, requires then the disarmament of prejudice on both sides. English-speaking Lutherans must abandon anti-Lutheran prejudices as to religious customs and usages, which they have acquired from Calvinistic associations, and must learn to judge more charitably, and with warmer appreciation of their foreign Lutheran brethren. And foreign-speaking Lutherans must abandon their unreasonable and narrow prejudice that the great historic Lutheran Church was meant to be restricted alone to their particular language, which would involve its inevitable belittlement and destruction. And, instead of disparaging criticism, and going into anti-Lutheran Churches in preference to those of their own faith, they should appreciate the sacrifices, and the heroism displayed by pastors and laymen, in seeking to build up the Lutheran Church in the English language.

And thus all yoke-fellows of the Lutheran household working harmoniously together, without regard to linguistic antecedents and prejudices, this vexatious rock of offence will at last be removed. And there will result a distinctively American Lutheran Church. A Church which, while preserving the characteristic faith and customs of the universal Lutheran Church, yet is in harmony with American spirit and life. For, just as the Lutheran Church in Germany has a Germanic type that is not of its essence, and in Scandinavia has a type resulting from the Scandinavian character, so will and must it be eventually here. The Lutheran Church, not in its foreign, but in an American phase, molded in nonessentials by, and harmonized with American institutions and character, is what must be the final resultant on our shores.

CHAPTER XXI.
THE LUTHERAN A WORLD-WIDE, OR TRULY CATHOLIC CHURCH.

THE Lutheran Church is not only the oldest, but also the greatest of Protestant Churches. Numerically, she far outstrips all others. In her general distribution, too, she maintains the same pre-eminence. The most distinctive and favorite term of the Christian Church in ancient times was Catholic, i.e., universal. The Jewish and Pagan religions were national. That is, they were particularistic, narrowed down to a particular race or class. There was one religion for the Jew and another for the Greek; one for the freeman and another for the slave; one for the aristocrats and another for the menial classes. But it was the distinguishing glory of Christianity that it abolished all these social and race distinctions. It broke down the barriers that separated men into antagonistic parties. The Apostle could boast: "There is neither Jew nor Greek, there is neither bond nor free; for you are all one in Christ Jesus" (Gal. 3:28). That is, the Christian is the one universal, or Catholic religion.

Now this primal condition of Christianity is reproduced alone in the Evangelical Lutheran Church. It is the Catholic, among the Protestant Churches. Its distribution is literally world-wide. While the greatest of the other Protestant denominations is the Established Church in but a single country, the Lutheran is the Established or National Church in about thirty-five of the governments of the world. Notable among these are Prussia,[125] Saxony, Bavaria, Hanover, Mecklenburg, Wurtemberg, Hamburg, Alsace-Lorraine, Denmark, Danish West Indies, Sweden, Norway, Faroe Islands, Finland,

---

[125]Predominantly Lutheran, though united with the Reformed.

Iceland, etc., etc. In other countries, as in Hungary, the Baltic Provinces of Russia, Poland, Lapland, Holland, France, Great Britain, and the United States, she has a very large part of the Christian membership. So, over Asia, Africa and Oceanica—as Australia, New Zealand, the Fiji Islands, etc.—her vast ecclesiastical household extends.

It may literally be said, therefore, that there is not a continent, country, or island of the sea, where this Mother Church of Protestantism does not hold up the cross of Jesus, and offer the bread and water of life to the souls of men. "From the rising of the sun unto the going down thereof" (Psalm 1, 1) reaches her vast dominion. The Lutheran Church, too, repeats the miracle of Pentecost, by preaching the gospel in myriad languages. She is the polyglot Church, the Church of many tongues. In this world-wide communion she embraces no less than seventeen reigning sovereigns, and a membership of more than fifty millions.

Zockler's "Religious Statistics of the World" gives the number of Lutherans as 47,000,000, that of the Episcopalians as about 30,000,000, Presbyterians and Congregationalists together 25,000,000, besides a number of smaller denominations as the Methodists, Baptists, etc. But the latest statistical tables of Lutherans are as follows:

Germany, - - 28,272,000
Sweden, - - - 5,000,000
Denmark, Iceland, etc., 2 369,696
Norway, - 2,125,000
Russia, Finland, Poland, etc., 5,048,000
Other European Countries, 216,000
Asia, - - 113,000
Africa, - - - 122,976
Oceanica, - - 103,700
America, - - 7,107,800
50,478,172

Zockler puts the number of Protestants in the world at 150,000,000, while Rand & McNally's "Atlas of the World" makes it 108,000,000. According to the former, the Lutherans are immensely the leading denomination numerically, while if the latter estimate be correct, their number would almost equal that of all the other Protestants combined. Think of this vast army of 50,000,000 of Christians upholding the Lutheran banner, from Arctic Greenland to Tropical Australia, from land to land, and from sea to sea! Verily the Churches of the Augsburg Confession engirdle the globe. "Their line is gone out through all the earth, and their words to the end of the world" (Psalm 19:4).

Is not, this, then a world-wide—a truly Catholic Church? And what has given the Lutheran Church this universal distribution, this general establishment, this door of entrance to all peoples and tongues, is her genuine Catholicity of spirit. There is nothing narrow, one-sided, bigoted in her genius. Bound alone by God's Word, she is free, open, and many-sided in her polity and life. She does not make essentials of things secondary and indifferent. She makes a test of nothing that is not Scriptural. Forms of Church government, rites and ceremonies of worship, questions of casuistry, etc., which in other denominations are often made tests of conscience and communion, the Lutheran Church justly relegates to the sphere of Christian liberty.

Thus, insisting alone upon those conditions which the Scriptures have made fundamental, the Lutheran Church by her large Catholicity commends herself to widely varying classes and races of men. She adapts herself equally to the German and the English, the Scandinavian and the Slavonic, the Finn and the Lapp, the High and the Low Ecclesiastic, the Monarchist and the Republican, the learned and the simple. It is this broad, generic character, which accounts for her world-wide prevalence and popularity, and it is this which gives her that feature which should ever be the distinguishing mark of the Church of Christ, viz. that she is truly Catholic, or universal.

CHAPTER XXII.
UNPARALLELED GROWTH IN THE UNITED STATES.

DEEP as is the interest and just as is the pride we feel in the world-wide greatness of our beloved Church, her condition and prosperity in this our native land, are still of more intense interest to us. Her beginnings in America were very feeble. The first Lutherans came to America in 1621 from Holland, and were persecuted and repressed by the Dutch, so that it was fifty years before they were allowed to build an house of worship. This, one of the first Lutheran edifices in America, was erected about 1663, but soon torn down and succeeded by a plain log building, at the corner of Broadway and Rector Street, New York City, in 1684. In the year 1638 some Swedish Lutheran emigrants arrived and founded the Churches on the Delaware, which later were absorbed by the Episcopalians. These Swedes immediately upon landing built near Lewes, Delaware, "the first Evangelical Lutheran Church on this continent."

Shortly after, the emigration of German Lutherans began. And by the year 1710 they were coming in large numbers. In 1734 the sharp persecution of the Lutherans of Salzburg, drove them out of the fatherland, and a large colony settled in Georgia, on the Savannah River, near the city of Savannah. Pennsylvania, however, became the center of German Lutheran emigration. By the year 1750, the Lutheran population of the colony of Pennsylvania numbered 60,000 souls.

The Lutherans, however, were under the greatest disadvantages. Speaking a strange tongue, poor and uninfluential, and destitute of pastors, Churches, and schools, their spiritual condition was deplorable. Scattered as sheep without a shepherd, and unable to compete with the stronger and native denominations, it was inevitable that they and their children should largely become the prey of the sects around them. No wonder, then, that when the patriarch Muhlenberg arrived in 1842, his heart was so depressed as almost to despair of the outlook. But what a mighty ecclesiastical organization has been developed from this seemingly hopeless beginning!

The following table shows the marvelous changes in the century from Muhlenberg's death to the present.

In 1748 Muhlenberg organized the first Lutheran Synod, composed of but seven clerical members. Now there are 4 General synods, about 100 district and sub-synods, 5,000 ministers, nearly 10,000 Churches, and, if the statistics were all accurately gathered, about 1,500,000 communicants. This growth is altogether unparalleled by that of any other ecclesiastical body in the United States. The Government Census for 1890, in giving the comparative growth of the religious denominations in the United States for the last decade, shows that the Lutherans have increased in membership 487,000 and that the percentage of increase is as follows: Lutherans, 68 per cent., Episcopalians, 48 per cent., Presbyterians, 39 per cent, Baptists, 37 per cent, Congregationalists, 33 per cent, Methodists, 30 per cent. The Government Census further shows that in growth of Church property the Lutheran Church has outstripped in the same ratio the other five leading denominations. In 1840, Lutheran Church property amounted in value to but the insignificant sum of $2,854,286, while in 1890 it had risen to $34,218,234. The average value of Church buildings in the General Synod and General Council is $7,007.50, the highest average of any denomination in the United States. During the last decade there were erected 3,064 Lutheran Churches. It will not do to talk of Christianity declining, when there is one denomination in our country, which builds upon an average a new Church every working day in the week. Commenting on these figures, Rev. Dr. Carrol, the Government official for taking the religious census, says in the Independent: "The growth of the Lutheran Church during the decade last past has been phenomenal. While the rate of increase in the entire population since 1880, has been a fraction over 28 per cent., the Lutheran Church has increased by 68 per cent., or more than twice the rate of increase of the population of the country."

This amazing numerical and material growth has been largely owing to emigration. But no less extraordinary also has been the intensive growth. The first periodical was The Lutheran Observer, published in 1831, in the English language. Now there are 150 Lutheran periodicals, divided among the languages as follows: 55 English, 51 German, 17 Norwegian, 16 Swedish, 4 Danish, 1 Icelandic, 4 Finnish, 1 French, and 1 Hungarian. In 1832 the first college—Pennsylvania College—was founded; now there are 32 Lutheran colleges, with upwards of 5,000 students. In 1815, Hartwick Seminary was our solitary theological school, now there are 26 Lutheran theological seminaries with nearly 1,000 students for the ministry. Besides these, there are 10 Young Ladies' Seminaries, and 12 Academies, and 66 Orphans' Homes and Institutions of mercy. The growth in the publication interests has kept pace with other advances. It has not been long since Lutheran readers, Sunday Schools, etc., were largely dependent upon non-Lutheran religious publications. But 20 publication houses, many of them large and prosperous, now send forth an abundant supply of distinctively Lutheran literature.

And most notable of all has been the growth in benevolence. As the Church is advancing from poverty to comparative wealth, every branch of the Church shows rapid strides in this respect. This increased progress is also doubtless largely owing to the application of systematic methods in the raising of funds. The "Hand Book of Lutheranism" places the Synodical contributions for benevolence for 1890, at $848,324. With this amount no less than 2,162 mission congregations and stations have been maintained in our rapidly expanding Home Mission field. The great States and Territories of the West are filling up more largely with Lutherans than any others. Foreign Missions are maintained in India, Africa, and Japan, for which larger amounts are appropriated every year.[126] Individual

[126] The contributions to the single cause of Foreign Missions, for the biennium closing with 1892, made by the General Synod alone, with but one-seventh of the Lutheran membership of the country, amounted to $105.127.000.

beneficence is growing, as is shown by the more frequent and liberal gifts and bequests to the benevolent agencies of the Church. The unparalleled growth of the Lutheran Church in the United States, in all these respects, is a matter of surprise and solicitude to our brethren of other households. Surveying the ecclesiastical horoscope, they marvel at this "rising denomination," this "new ecclesiastical star" of the first magnitude, ascending the religious firmament. But there is nothing either startling or strange in the phenomenon. It is simply that the Mother of Protestantism is preparing to enfold all her children in her arms. It is that the leading Church of the old world is coming on, step by step, to take possession of the new.

And while this marvelous growth must thrill every Lutheran heart, what responsibilities it devolves upon each conscientious member! Seasons of growth are critical seasons—times of opportunity and labor. Never was there such an obligation laid upon the Lutherans of any country or age, as upon those of the rapidly developing Church in the United States. May they have the energy, the judiciousness, and the consecration, to be equal to the hour!

CHAPTER XXIII.
LOYALTY TO THE LUTHERAN CHURCH.

PATRIOTIC loyalty—love of one's native land—, and domestic loyalty—devotion to one's own home—, are justly esteemed among the first virtues. How much stronger reason, then, is there for Church loyalty—unswerving fidelity to our ecclesiastical mother, the Church which gave us spiritual birth, and tenderly nursed and fostered us to spiritual maturity. If the traitor and the filial ingrate be shunned among men, what shall we say of the one who despises his parental Church, and deliberately spurns his own ecclesiastical household and family! Accordingly, devotion to our mother Church is one of the most sacred Christian obligations. Phillips Brooks well said that "the man who loves the universal Church the most, will be the truest to his own particular Church." [127] It is the one whose religious convictions are*vague and superficial, who is ever ready to cry that one Church is as good as another. Loyalty to our own Church does not keep us from loving and appreciating Christians of other households, but it does demand that we love ours the more, and give to it our respect, our service, and our defense. There are Churches we could name whose members are remarkable for this unfaltering fidelity, and what vantage of strength and influence it gives them!

The degree of our loyalty naturally depends upon the character of that object which calls it forth. Thus, American patriotism should be exceptionally strong on account of the singular glory of his country which thrills the breast of every true American with pride. And so the Church love of the Lutheran has more stirring reasons to incite it, than that of any other. Writes one of our most

---

[127] Yale Lectures on Preaching, p. 227.

intelligent laymen: "We have in our Lutheran Church, doctrine that is pure, a refinement and good taste exhibited in her forms and services that must satisfy the most fastidious, and a history to which all Christendom does homage. Let us love it; and

let us show our faith by our works."[128] How true this is? Where is the Church whose faith can stand the test of Scripture as ours, or that has behind it so illustrious a history? And ought not these considerations to inspire within the hearts of her children emotions of unequalled love and pride?

And yet, what are the facts? It must be confessed, we fear, that perhaps no Church in America seems to have so light a hold upon her sons and daughters as the Lutheran. How many are always ready to look up to other Churches, while disposed to regard disdainfully their own. And how common it is for Lutherans to be ready to seize the slightest occasion to sever the bonds that hold them to their own Church! How many Lutherans there are who do not honor and revere their own historic characteristics, and instead of holding them up for others to imitate, are ever eager to be copying from others. How often, too, when a prejudice is found to exist against an honored Lutheran usage, the disposition is to defer too greatly to it. Whereas, the only successful way to disarm prejudice against a rightful custom is by its courageous use. Such a manly course will at once demonstrate the groundlessness of the objection, and bring honor upon the Church and its practices.

Why is it that we have sustained such incalculable losses from time to time, and that in the great cities we are not in the lead as we should be? It is largely on account of the flaccid fiber of so much of Lutheran loyalty. It is because of that lack of Church love which springs from lack of character and intelligence. "A man with a heart," said Frederick William III. to Napoleon, "will remember the cradle in which he was rocked when a child." So, a want of Church loyalty springs primarily from the defect of religious principle, and the lack of a true self-respect. But, secondarily, it proceeds from the want of

---

[128] St. James' Lenten Messenger, New York, 1888.

knowledge. It is more frequently ignorance than anything else that causes many nominal Lutherans to regard slightingly the Lutheran Church, and to be holding others in esteem above it. "There was a time when the dominant tendency was to glory that we are like everybody, and consequently nothing in ourselves, living by mere sufferance, despised by others as those having little respect for themselves. Suddenly, as the cloud lifted, the great proportions of our Church, her vast heritage, her wonderful structure of theology, her rich treasures in every department of religious literature, and her active work in so many spheres of beneficence, come to view. How easy now to glory that we are Lutherans!"[129] Intelligent people in other Churches need not be told of the Lutheran Church, and are accustomed to look up to it with the greatest respect. It is a sad commentary therefore on the ignorance of our own members, when they are deficient in esteem and love for the house of their faith and of their fathers.

A higher type of Lutheran Church loyalty is then one of our most imperative needs. It is not numbers but quality—unfaltering devotion—that makes a Church efficient and progressive. In a crisis of unwonted peril, Caesar would lean upon none but his famous tenth legion, because he knew he could trust their loyalty to the last. They would die before they would betray or dishonor the Roman standard. So Lutherans, while not disparaging, or thinking uncharitably of any other Church, should cling to their own Church, bear high its standard, defend it from misrepresentation, and do and sacrifice for it, with a devotion that knows no tire.

The scroll of Lutheran Church history is emblazoned with some of the brightest examples of Church love that shed honor upon Christendom. And so, let us trust that the era of Lutheran indifference, denominational laxity, and want of self-respect in our American Lutheran Church, if. reaching the stage of "innocuous desuetude." All signs indicate rather that a new epoch is upon us when the old adage will be proven, "once a Lutheran, always a

---

[129] Introduction to "Lutherans in America," p. 10.

Lutheran." And when no other denomination of Christians can boast a stronger and more uncompromising Church love than that which characterizes an Evangelical Lutheran. When Lutheran parents feel a deep solicitude that their children should perpetuate their family name in honorable place in the Lutheran Church, and when Lutheran sons and daughters feel that it is a tribute of willing reverence to their parents to abide in the spiritual house of their fathers, then will our numerous losses cease, and will our beloved Church have pride and not humiliation in her children.

Assault who may, kiss and betray,
Dishonor and disown,
My Church shall still be dear to me —
My fathers' and my own!

CHAPTER XXIV.
FUTURE OF THE LUTHERAN CHURCH IN AMERICA.

WHEN we bear in mind how conspicuously the Lutheran is the leading Protestant Church of Europe, and how phenomenal her recent growth has been in America, we are naturally disposed to raise the question, "What shall be her future in this Western World?" We have seen that during the last decade the Lutheran Church has increased at a ratio more than twice that of the increase of the population of the country. If this ratio of progress continues, it is evident that a very great future destiny is before us. But this future largely depends upon our denominational wisdom or folly. In the past our blunders have been almost as phenomenal as our advance, so that we have grown, as it were, in spite of ourselves. Everyone knows that our losses have been almost incalculable, and that other denominations have largely flourished upon our best material. Patrick Henry said he knew of no other lamp by which to guide his feet onward than the lamp of experience. And so, a study of the causes that have hindered our progress in the past, and cost us such great losses, will best serve to guard us against these mistakes in the future. To make, then, the most of the rare denominational opportunity which Providence has placed in our hands, let us note these lessons.

First, let us repress fraternal strife, and inter-synodical prejudices, jealousies, and contentions. And, bound together by the tie of Lutheran unity, let all work together with the common purpose to advance our beloved Zion.

Let us, too, frown down, what a prominent German Lutheran minister has aptly termed "the linguistic devil." Let it rather be a glory to our Church that she is the Church of many tongues, than to make it a theme of reproach and an apple of discord. Let not the German or Scandinavian entertain the bigoted thought that Lutheranism is limited to his narrow native tongue, and that one cannot be a Lutheran if he uses the English language. And he who founds an English Lutheran Church, must not commit the equally grave error, of seeking to establish a totally new Church, rejecting that historic faith and those historic usages, without which the Church he frames has no claim whatever to the title Lutheran. In short, the Church in America must be Lutheran, and not something else. And it must more and more largely every year, and eventually altogether, use the English language. A Church in a foreign tongue can never come into thorough contact with the life of a people. And such an un-American Church will be but a diminishing influence, and ever have a more and more languishing life. Our Church's future in this land depends most largely upon the good commonsense with which our foreign-speaking Lutherans will adapt themselves to the situation, and upon their loyally bringing up their sons and daughters in English Lutheran Churches. An unnatural effort to retain them in a Church with a foreign tongue, or indifferently allowing them to go to a non-Lutheran Church, will but repeat the regretful story of the past. "There is no reason why, if properly administered, the Lutheran Church should not be as influential in this country, as any religious communion that has found a home here. But to attain this end, some very important factors must be regarded. The Church feeling as distinguished from the merely congregational must be diligently cultivated, and our people must learn that the interests of the Church are far more important than those of any congregation. Then the Lutheran Church feeling must also be asserted. We must build upon our own distinctive doctrines, worship according to our own Orders of Service, be governed by our own polity, and cultivate our own form of Christian life. The secret of the failures of some men in the Lutheran ministry, is that they have never understood the peculiar spirit of the Lutheran Church, and could not, therefore, build up Lutheran congregations. The secret of the lack of success of many congregations is that they have attempted to provide for Lutheran people according to measures that they have seen practiced with seeming success in other denominations. The proper rule for Churches as well as for individuals, is: 'Be yourself, if you would gain respect.' This is especially true, when consistency involves no disgrace, but is the highest honor."[130]

Another error of great significance to be avoided in the future, is our neglect to hold the great municipal centers. Our principal strength is in the smaller towns and country, and our chief weakness is in the great cities. And as those cities are the very heart of the nation, whence the- currents of life and influence radiate in all directions, those who control them hold the keys of the future. We have the country; we have large numbers; what should now be our aim is to have strong Churches in the leading municipal centers. This will give our Church that prominence, wealth, culture, and influence, which are invaluable aids to denominational prosperity, piety, usefulness, and power.

Profiting, thus, by her sore experiences in the past, and improving, by liberality and zeal, the exceptional opportunity and responsibility given her, the future for the Lutheran Church in this land is a most auspicious one. It must be borne in mind also that the conditions are far more favorable to her now than they formerly were. Her German origin, once a hindrance and reproach, now that the German mind is the acknowledged intellectual master and preceptor of civilization, is a credit and stimulus to her. For a long period of our country's history, too, the predominance of the Puritanic type in American Christianity was most unfavorable to an historic and liturgical Church. But the wonderful change in this respect, so that the whole tide is setting powerfully in favor of the Churchly denominations, makes that which once was a detriment now a signal advantage. The historic Church, the Church whose faith and practice are rooted in the past, it now appears beyond all doubt, is to be the Church of the future. For as there is a spiritual unity binding together the Christian ages, so in the true Church of Christ universal, 'jast, present, and future, must meet in one. And as the Lutheran has the best, and richest, and most glorious history, this is a vital point in her favor.

[130] The Lutheran, April 8, 1893.

Moreover, as the Lutheran Church gave to the world that civil and religious liberty, which is the peculiar glory of our institutions, the genius of Lutheranism is especially adapted to the spirit of America. And, as then, the Lutheran Church was the founder of the pure phase of modern Christianity, so let us trust that in the very forefront of those Christian columns which are here, under the guidance of God, working out the last and highest problems of human destiny, will gleam the standard of our beloved Evangelical Lutheran Church.

Made in the USA
Charleston, SC
26 November 2014